EDWIN GINN

Seventy Years
of Textbook Publishing

A History of Ginn and Company

BY

THOMAS BONAVENTURE LAWLER

1867 · 1937

OMNIA CORRUMPUNTUR ET INTABESCUNT IN TEMPORE;
SATURNUS QUOS GENERAT DEVORARE NON CESSAT;
OMNEM MUNDI GLORIAM OPERIRET OBLIVIO,
NISI DEUS MORTALIBUS LIBRORUM REMEDIA PROVIDISSET.
[RICHARD DE BURY, PHILOBIBLON. 1345, A.D.]

All things are corrupted and decay in time;
Saturn ceases not to devour the children that he generates;
all the glory of the world would be buried in oblivion,
if God had not provided mortals with the remedy of books.

GINN AND COMPANY
BOSTON · NEW YORK · CHICAGO
LONDON · ATLANTA · DALLAS · COLUMBUS · SAN FRANCISCO

Z
473
G4 L4

TO MY PARTNERS IN THE FIRM

PAST AND PRESENT

IN DEEP APPRECIATION

OF HAPPY YEARS

◇

PREFACE

IN THE course of seventy years the firm of Ginn and Company has published thousands of text-books, covering many branches of education. This history of the house cannot, of course, tell the story of all these works. Some were published to meet conditions that in the event proved to be somewhat ephemeral. They had their day, and ceased to be. Of these books we might say with Virgil to Dante,

Non ragioniam di lor, ma guarda e passa.[1]

As full consideration as possible, however, has been given to epoch-making authors and their works. As one scans the list, it cannot be gainsaid that the house secured as its authors a very large number of the leaders in numerous branches of educational activity, profound scholars and progressive teachers of college and school. The house has endeavored to be a vital force in the promotion of texts that develop the human mind. Its aim has been to inspire in the child a desire for knowledge, culture, and character, and the determination to have a share in building up for the nation a worthy citizenship.

No book of this type would be complete without a somewhat comprehensive personal record of the members of the firm, who have worked so unceasingly for the success of the house during the eventful years of its history.

The editorial department has furnished us with

[1]"Let us not speak of them, but look and pass" (*Inferno*, iii, 51).

vii

outstanding and often epoch-making works to record the advance of human knowledge. The mental grasp of the members of this department is a source of wonder and gratitude on the part of authors whose manuscripts have come under their critical but kindly eyes.

I would pay my tribute of praise to the large force of agents, who, like the couriers described by Herodotus, have carried on their work in snow, and rain, and heat, and gloom of night, to secure the introductions of books into the schools, a devotion without which no success for the firm could have been possible. Their number is too great for special mention, but their loyalty to the house has ever been a source of deep appreciation.

I would also pay my meed of praise to the members of the Ginn staff — in the Press and in the offices throughout the land — whose intelligent activities have given, as I believe, enduring testimony of their prompt and efficient service.

The author is greatly indebted to his partner Henry Hoyt Hilton, whose long membership in the firm and remarkable memory of events have added many facts of import about men and policies during the last half-century of textbook-publishing.

T. B. L.

CONTENTS

[13]

[x]

[xi]

Seventy Years
of Textbook Publishing

THE

ENGLISH OF SHAKESPEARE;

ILLUSTRATED IN

A Philological Commentary

ON HIS

JULIUS CÆSAR.

BY

GEORGE L. CRAIK,

PROFESSOR OF HISTORY AND OF ENGLISH LITERATURE IN QUEEN'S COLLEGE,
BELFAST.

Edited, from the Third Revised London Edition,

BY

W. J. ROLFE,

MASTER OF THE HIGH SCHOOL, CAMBRIDGE, MASS.

BOSTON

EDWIN GINN

CHAPTER ONE

◇

A YEAR
OF STORM AND STRESS

THE YEAR 1867, in which the house of Ginn was founded, has been called by a historian the nadir of the American republic. At last the War between the States was over, but what followed was almost as bad as the war itself. Lincoln was in his grave, and the South was exposed to the ruthless hands of the " carpetbaggers," who swept away the most picturesque civilization in the nation's history.

Under the rule of the radicals in Washington ten former Confederate States of the South were divided into five military satrapies, over each of which an army officer exercised the strictest military rule. The leading men of these states were disqualified for public office, and four million slaves were set free and were soon given the right of the ballot. The spoilsmen of the North and the illiterate freedmen of the South, in a riot of anarchy and robbery, imposed on this impoverished people a war debt of more than $300,000,000. Never before in the history of the country had the government at Washington reached the depth to which it had now descended.

The distant country beyond the Mississippi River, still the home of Indians and buffaloes, was just beginning to receive its influx of settlers, who, in their canvas-covered prairie schooners, drawn by oxen, horses, or mules, pursued their slow way, beset hourly by difficulties and dangers.

But soon a telegraph line was extended across the Great Plains; and now was heard the thud of the

[5]

sledge hammers driving the spikes of the new railroad, one end extending from Omaha westward, and the other extending from Sacramento eastward, while through the Sierras and the Rockies tunnels were being blasted. In the meantime the Pony Express and the passenger coaches continued to make their dusty trips across the boundless prairies.

Chicago was a frontier city of about two hundred and fifty thousand inhabitants. Commerce in wheat, lumber, and food products made it the fastest-growing community of the country. It had learned the secret of packing beef and pork. Armour and Morris were sending meat products to the Eastern States and far beyond, to England and the continent of Europe. Swift was later to show the advantages of the refriger-ator system for shipping dressed beef.

The McCormick self-binding reaper and harvester was pushing the line of civilization westward thirty miles a year. The great flour mills of Minnesota were beginning to take their place in the forefront of the milling industry, using the power of the falls discov-ered by Father Hennepin nearly two centuries before.

The oil business had begun its wonderful develop-ment after the earlier discovery of Colonel Drake. The sudden rapid progress of 1865 in western Penn-sylvania was the beginning of a new era in industrial history that was destined to involve the fate of nations.

St. Louis had been active with the commerce of the packet boats moored along the water front of the great Mississippi, after completing the dangerous journey to and from New Orleans. But the railroads were already sealing the doom of this river traffic. The great Eads Bridge across the Mississippi was in process of erection.

In 1867 the population of the United States was about thirty-six million. There were thirty-seven states in the Union. Nebraska had been admitted in that year; and Alaska, whose size was one fifth of the entire United States, had been bought from Russia for the small sum of $7,200,000.

The country had never seen or heard of electric lights, telephones, Diesel engines, airplanes, typewriters, typesetting machines, radio, automobiles, antiseptic surgery, internal-combustion motors, cocaine, submarines, serums, X rays, radium, 200-inch telescopes, television, or teletype. Nor did it have poison gas, "Big Berthas," and bombing planes.

The nation, despite the activities of the politicians in Washington, saw the beginning of rapid business developments, a boom for the Northern States. Factories and mills were being built in great numbers; cities were growing by leaps and bounds; and immigrants were pouring in, more than a quarter of a million a year, to secure for themselves and their children land that was denied them in the countries of Europe. A hundred thousand of these immigrants pushed on every year to the West and settled beyond the Mississippi, even though at the time there were frequent wars with the Indians. Added to these troubles were plagues of grasshoppers, tornadoes, blizzards, and battles between cattlemen and sheepmen. The barbed-wire fence and the Colt revolver were destined to change the life and the customs of the Great Plains.

In American literature Longfellow, Lowell, Whittier, Motley, Whitman, Parkman, Bret Harte, and Mark Twain were adding to American letters. Dickens had finished most of his famous novels, and was at this time on a second successful visit to the United States. His great English fellow novelist, Thackeray, had passed away only four years earlier.

Education had made progress in the nation, but at a snail's pace. The first public normal school had been established in Lexington, Massachusetts, twenty-eight years before this time. There were now about forty training schools for teachers. Forty years earlier Horace Mann had been elected secretary of the State Board of Education of Massachusetts, and began his memorable work, believing, as he said, in the accelerating improvability of men. Illiteracy was so widespread that nearly one fourth of the white people of the country could neither read nor write. One year later citizenship was granted to the former slaves, and in 1870 the right of suffrage to four million illiterate freedmen.

Five years earlier the first Morrill Act had been passed. It promoted industrial education, manual

[8]

training, and vocational education, and was the basis of the land-grant colleges of the nation.

Articulation, fused courses, measuring scales, 6–3–3, skills, purposive education, educational plateaus, retardation, motivation, and socialized recitation were terms yet to be presented in the school world.

In Massachusetts compulsory education had been enacted into law only fifteen years earlier. On the statute books of most of the states it was still unwritten.

Horace, in one of his Odes, says that the man who first braved the seas in a frail vessel must have had a heart of brass and a nerve of steel. We might well think Edwin Ginn must have been similarly endowed when he decided, in the distressing year of 1867, to launch forth into the printing and publishing of textbooks. He was, as events proved, a man of vision and of great determination of purpose. He knew the almost passionate devotion of the American people to education; he foresaw the ultimate, peaceful reunion of the nation, the growth of an outstanding industrial activity, and the development of the vast region of the West, as the frontier was pushed ever forward and new states were added to the Union. In his vision he saw millions of children trooping to the elementary schools throughout the land and the tens of thousands of earnest students who would be enrolled in the high schools and in the state and private colleges that, he rightfully believed, would soon be rising in all parts of the Union.

[9]

To meet the needs of these children and of the high-school and college students, Edwin Ginn decided to go forward with his plans. The year 1867 saw the establishment of the Federal Bureau of Education in Washington, a happy augury, perhaps, for a new publishing house devoted exclusively to educational textbooks.

CHAPTER TWO

◇

EDWIN GINN

EDWIN GINN, son of James and Sarah Blood Ginn, was born in 1838, on a farm in the town of Orland, Maine. The Ginn family was descended from a James Ginn, who came from England to Virginia about the year 1700. A part of the family came north and settled in Maine. It was there that Edwin Ginn's grandfather received a commission from the governor of Massachusetts:

" By His Excellency
" John Hancock, Esq.
" Governor of the Commonwealth of
" Massachusetts
" To James Ginn, Gentleman, Greeting
" You being appointed Captain of the first Com-
" pany, in the fifth Regiment, and in the second Bri-
" gade of the eighth Division of the Militia of this Com-
" monwealth, Comprehending the County of Lincoln.
" By virtue of the power vested in me, I do by these
" Presents (Reposing special trust and confidence in
" your Loyalty, Courage and good Conduct) Com-
" mission you accordingly. You are therefore care-
" fully and diligently to discharge the duty of a
" Captain in leading, ordering, and exercising said
" Company in Arms, both inferior officers and sol-
" diers; and to keep them in good order and disci-
" pline; and they are hereby commanded to obey
" you as their Captain and you are yourself to observe
" and follow such orders and instructions as you shall
" from time to time receive from me or your superior
" officers.

[13]

"Given under my hand and the seal of the said "Commonwealth the twenty ninth day of August in "the year of our Lord, 1787, and of the independence "of the United States of America the twelfth.

"By his Excellency's Command.

"John Avery Jun. Sect."

"My father's farm [Edwin wrote] was remarkably productive of stones, both small and large, and every spring it was my good fortune to strengthen my back by picking them up. It used to fall to the lot of my brother and myself to pile the stones in little round heaps, two or three feet in diameter. Of course we were glad when haying came, for then we had a change of occupation. I spread hay, cut firewood, took care of the horses, cows, and sheep, and drew water, sometimes when the thermometer was twenty degrees below zero. At this time I was only seven years old."

At the age of twelve young Edwin in his vacation went to a logging camp as cook.

"The men never went hungry [he wrote]. We had pork and beans, good bread with pork fat and molasses for butter, and both salt and fresh meat, though not much else; but all of us thrived on this bill of fare."

Later he went on a deep-sea codfishing schooner to the Grand Banks of Newfoundland, where for weeks the little vessel was out of sight of land. Northeast gales swept the waves over the small schooner,

[14]

or the dense fog wrapped her in darkness for days. He later called these trips "summer excursions or summer schools." They were better than elementary courses in physical geography; for he acquired more knowledge about the tides, winds, ocean currents, fogs, and shore lines, not to mention what he learned about fishing, than books could tell him.

His earliest school days were spent in a little red schoolhouse on a bleak New England hillside. The school continued two months in summer and two in winter. He later attended Bucksport Seminary, two miles and a half from his home, and walked both ways. Later he attended Westbrook Seminary, where he roomed with a young man whose father was engaged in the publishing of textbooks. This happy association proved a turning point in the boy's life, as the father of his roommate gave him an opportunity to secure work in a publishing house.

In 1858, at the age of twenty, Edwin Ginn entered Tufts College. In the middle of his college course he strained his eyes, and for a time was unable to use them; but he wouldn't give up, and made arrangements with several of his classmates to read to him. Despite this handicap, he passed his examinations and graduated with his class.

Confronted now with an indebtedness of twelve hundred dollars, he started at once to wipe out his debts by selling textbooks on commission, and within a year found himself even with the world.

One of the houses for which he worked was that of Clark and Maynard, who published Anderson's *History of the United States* and the unusually successful Reed and Kellogg *Language Lessons*. Mr. Ginn secured the adoption of Anderson's history for the city of Boston. Another house for which he worked was Crosby and Ainsworth; but he had an aversion to working on a salary. His reason for it is today not hard to see. Besides the usual five senses given to man, he had two more — common sense and vision. He saw visions, and he dreamed dreams, and he wished to have a business of his own.

◇

CHAPTER THREE

THE BEGINNING OF THE FIRM

I N 1867 one of the members of the Crosby and Ainsworth house became interested in Ginn's plan of having a publishing house of his own, and suggested to him that he might buy Craik's *English of Shakespeare*, which they published, as a nucleus of his business.

Mr. Ginn had a deep appreciation of good literature, and was himself particularly interested in Shakespeare, which he believed might, with proper textbooks, well become an active subject in the high schools and colleges throughout the land. Professor George L. Craik, author of the *English of Shakespeare*, was a professor of history and of English literature in Queen's College, Belfast. Mr. Ginn bought the book as the basis of English in his publishing house, and said that he planned to improve the schools by putting into the hands of the youth better books than those already in use. In 1869 the Harvard Catalogue announced that students might prepare themselves for entrance in English by using Craik's *English of Shakespeare* or Milton's *Comus*.

The name of his publishing house was simply Edwin Ginn. An elder brother soon joined the firm, and the name became Ginn Brothers. Aaron Lovell, a classmate of Mr. Ginn's at Tufts College, and Robert F. Leighton, who had received his doctorate at Leipzig and was now principal of the Melrose High School, became partners in 1870, the firm name being changed to Ginn Brothers and Company.

A few years later Mr. Ginn bought the Lovell and Leighton interests, and the firm name reverted to Ginn Brothers. Except for a brief time, Fred B. Ginn was a member of the firm until his death, in 1907.

In 1873 Daniel C. Heath, a native of Farmington, Maine, and a graduate of Amherst College, became an agent for Mr. Ginn, with his headquarters at Rochester, New York. He had been a high-school principal and was well versed in the methods of the schoolroom. In 1876 he became a partner, and the firm name was changed to Ginn and Heath. At this time Mr. Heath joined Mr. Ginn in the Boston office.

In his early youth Edwin Ginn had learned to appreciate the best in the world's literature. He once wrote in a letter:

" This morning I took up my *Plutarch's Lives*. After glancing at several of the characters, I hit upon Cato the Younger, and it seemed like renewing my youth. The companionship of those great men, under the guidance of such a master as Plutarch, is rejuvenating. It makes one's ordinary routine seem extremely commonplace, and creates the desire to give more time to the things that make life worth living. It has been my habit always to dwell for two or three hours each day with great personages, the great philosophers of the ages."

Mr. Ginn wrote to Charles W. Eliot, Charles Eliot Norton, Edward Everett Hale, and other prominent scholars, asking what literature they were wont to

[20]

place in the hands of their children to enable them to begin to understand a book as a whole. The result of these inquiries was the series called Classics for Children, books designed to cover the years of instruction in elementary schools.

The Classics for Children seemed at the time rather formidable: *Plutarch's Lives*, Scott's *Lady of the Lake*, Ruskin's *King of the Golden River*, Marcus Aurelius, *Robinson Crusoe*, Lamb's *Tales from Shakespeare*, Scott's *Tales of a Grandfather* and *Quentin Durward*, and *Don Quixote*. Mr. Ginn himself edited some of the books, as his letter above implies when he speaks of *my* Plutarch. In editing *The Lady of the Lake* he added a map to show the scene of the poem, intelligent footnotes, an excerpt from the *Tales of a Grandfather*, to show the manners and customs of the Highlanders and Borderers of Scotland, and a glossary of Scotch words. The Classics for Children, models of literary art, were an instant success. They had an important bearing on the development of supplementary reading in the schools, an idea now commonplace in elementary education.

Rousseau's *Émile* had a great influence in turning Mr. Ginn's mind to this series. In *Émile* we read:

" Since we must have books, there is one which, to my mind, furnishes the finest of treatises on education according to nature. My Émile shall read this book before any other; it shall for a long time be his entire library, and shall always hold an honorable place. It shall be the text on which all our discussions of natural science shall be only commentaries. It shall be a test for all we meet during our progress toward a ripened judgment; and so long as our taste is unspoiled, we shall enjoy reading it. What wonderful book is this? Aristotle? Pliny? Buffon? No. It is *Robinson Crusoe.*"

The insistence put by some progressive city-school superintendents on required reading, and study of six standard classics by each child before graduation from the grammar school, led Dr. Washington Gladden to write of it as follows:

"The benefit of such a course of reading as this may be very great. Plenty of trash finds its way into the hands of these boys and girls; but many of them there are who would never, but for some such requirement as this, make the acquaintance of any good book. If they can be taught to perceive the beauties of these English classics, to relish the great humor of Irving, and to find pleasure in the sound manliness of Scott, many of them may be saved from the mental debauchery offered by the newsstands."

Some years before this time Henry N. Hudson, a graduate of Middlebury College, had edited in eleven volumes the plays of Shakespeare, "the greatest name," says Hallam, "in all literature."

The Shakespeare venture had not been a success; and Hudson was glad to sell the plates to Mr. Ginn, who brought out, in two volumes, *Shakespeare: his Life, Art, and Characters,* a scholarly, detailed study of the history and works of the bard of Avon.

[22]

This was followed by the School Shakespeare, in twenty-three handy, well-bound volumes, each volume containing a play. Each play was introduced by a discussion of its history, the source of its plot, the political situation, and a critical estimate of the leading characters.

Hudson was a commanding figure, standing six feet four, straight as an Indian sachem, and a lover of the best things in literature. In his *Classical English Reader*, a collection of noble thoughts, which Ginn and Heath published, he gave this as his creed:

" Finally, no man having drunk the wine of old books, straightway desireth the new; for he saith the old is better. So old wine, old books, old friends, old songs, the precious music of the heart, are the wine, the books, the friends, the songs for me."

Hudson's Shakespeare quickly became a standard; and in later editions, with distinguished scholars as editors, the series is today a work of outstanding success. It might be described as an early success of the house.

As showing that the firm still invokes the spirit of Shakespeare for the development of the fuller study of English in school and college, it may be remarked that the magnum opus of Professor George Lyman Kittredge, covering all the works of Shakespeare, was published in sumptuous format by the house in 1936.

Mr. Ginn did not rely on his own judgment in the upbuilding of his list. At the very outset he began to correspond with the leading educational men of the land and to seek their aid and opinions. One of these men was Thomas Davidson, "one of the twelve greatest scholars of the world." Mr. Ginn nowhere gives a list of the other eleven. It was as a result of this policy of calling on great advisers that he wrote, "We have an imprint, the value of which cannot be overestimated." Progressive in his ideas, Mr. Ginn once drew attention to a saying of Horace Mann, the educator whose statue is on the lawn before the Statehouse of Massachusetts:

"Wherever I have found the best institutions, there I have always found the greatest desire to know how similar institutions are administered elsewhere; and where I have found the worst, there I have found most of the spirit of self-complacency and even an offensive disinclination to hear of better methods."

Some idea of the activity of the house may be obtained from the fact that during the first ten years ten books on Greek, fourteen on Latin, ten on music, two on geography, and twenty on miscellaneous subjects were published. Since the capital was small, these were years of trial in the matter of financing a growing business; but strenuous as the difficulties were, Edwin Ginn kept well ahead of them. At one time three men who had lent him money became somewhat alarmed at what they believed to be undue expansion. They decided to call at Mr. Ginn's office and take over the business, to protect their notes.

Mr. Ginn greeted them with a cheerful smile, and before they could broach their mission (the purpose of which Mr. Ginn at once divined), he said, " Gentlemen, I am glad you came today; for I wish to pay off your notes." From that day forward he never had any difficulty in financing his rapidly growing business, especially as he had in Mr. S. D. Warren, the great paper-manufacturer, a devoted friend who appreciated his purposes and was always glad to render him financial assistance.

From the very beginning Mr. Ginn planned to build up a strong corps of agents to cover every school and college of importance in the land. He insisted on " young graduates from college, taken on because of their integrity, honesty, and alertness."

Macaulay says a great ambition of Frederick William of Prussia was to form a brigade of giants, and every country was ransacked by his agents for men above the ordinary stature; no head that towered above the crowd in the bazaars of Aleppo, Cairo, or Surat was permitted to escape.

Not so interested merely in men of towering physique as was Frederick, the members of the firm, in recruiting their corps of agents, have ever been on the lookout for teachers of outstanding scholarship and acumen, who would prefer as a lifework the active sphere of business to the quieter atmosphere of school and college. With rare exceptions, therefore, the agency staff has been drawn from the classroom.

CHAPTER FOUR

◇

THE CLASSICAL ERA
LATIN

MR. GINN's mind being of a classical bent, he desired especially to meet the needs of high schools and colleges in the matter of the classics. At that time, as now, Latin was an important subject in education, and throughout the land it was required for the degree of Bachelor of Arts, in colleges as well as in the leading scientific schools.

In 1869 Professor William F. Allen of the University of Wisconsin had completed a brief *Latin Grammar*, which was published by Mr. Ginn. It ran through five editions in the first year, a remarkable success in view of there being already in use three Latin grammars written by distinguished professors. The new grammar had the essentials of Latin, with fewer details than the other grammars.

The success of Allen's *Latin Grammar* led Professor Thatcher of Yale to offer to Mr. Ginn, for publication, a translation of Madvig's *Latin Grammar*, which a leading authority pronounced to be the fullest and most profound Latin grammar ever published. Madvig was one of the great German philologists who dug down deep to find the roots of the Indo-European stock of languages.

Since a book of this nature could not find a place in the high schools or the small colleges, Mr. Ginn published it as a contribution to classical culture. It fitted into the plan devised by him for publishing from time to time works that would be a distinct contribution to education, though of little or no

[29]

monetary value to the house. It was, Mr. Ginn said, a duty of an educational publishing house to share in the production of such works.

In 1870, at the request of Mr. Ginn, Dr. Joseph H. Allen, a brother of Professor William F. Allen, author of the *Latin Grammar*, wrote a *Latin Primer*.

In the preface of this book the author expressed ideas which, in view of the present decline in the study of Latin and Greek, are interesting today.

"I do not see why [he says] intelligent children of ten or twelve, after the manner of forty or fifty years ago, should not learn Latin, and enjoy its simpler forms, which, indeed, seems the best possible introduction to a systematic course in school or college. But to secure this end, it must be taught, first of all, *as a living and flexible tongue*, not in the abstract principles and methods of its grammar; and secondly by familiar use in *narrative and dialogue*, not by committing to memory disjointed examples and dry forms. If we consent to regard it as a dead language, or study it as if it had no other than an antiquarian or scientific interest, we cannot long uphold the general study of it at all. An easy and familiar reading knowledge of a language is worth incomparably more to most students of it, than any supposed advantage in the study of its grammatical structure."

In Latin of his own composing, or in simplification of the Vulgate, Dr. Allen produced lessons running through the stories of the Bible, dialogues on everyday affairs, fables, stories from Herodotus, Pliny, and Hadrian, and nursery songs.

It might be interesting to see how Dr. Allen treats the simple nursery rhymes every child has heard:

Poor Robin Redbreast	*Rubicilla*
The North wind doth blow,	Stridet ventus Borealis,
And we shall have snow;	Imber ingruet nivalis;
And what will the Robin do then,	Quo se vertet horâ in illâ
Poor thing?	Rubicilla?
He'll sit in a barn,	In granario sedebit,
And keep himself warm,	Plumeâ tepens fovebit
And hide his head under his wing,	Molle caput sub axillâ,
Poor thing!	Rubicilla!

Latin can apparently be a living tongue for the nursery as well as for the Roman Senate, where Cicero thunders against the despoilers of Sicily.

In 1872 the name of James B. Greenough, a distinguished Latin scholar, was added to the list of Ginn authors. For the next forty years his name was on the title pages of the many Latin books published by the house. With Joseph H. Allen he revised the *Latin Grammar*, and they made practically a new book, the Allen and Greenough *Latin Grammar*. It was founded on comparative grammar, and gave the philology of the forms of Latin; it made use of the results of modern investigators, and probably for the first time a philosophical treatment of the subjunctive mood made it intelligible to the average high-school pupils and gave them a correct idea of the Latin protasis and apodosis. With the aid of Latin scholars and teachers there followed a list of high-school texts, under the name of Allen and Greenough, which were kept abreast of the times. The *Caesar* of these authors, revised by D'Ooge and Daniell, gave an idea of the progress made in teaching Latin. The mortality in second-year Latin was so great that Professor Greenough removed from *Caesar* some of the difficulties of Latin syntax by adding judicious references to the *Latin Grammar* and by presenting the indirect discourse of the thirteenth chapter of the first book in direct form. Professor Greenough had visited the scenes of the Gallic War; and to humanize the subject he introduced a special treatise on the art of war among the Romans, including maps and plans of battles, as well as pictures of persons, places, coins, and armor, with a detailed story of Caesar as a man and of the conditions in Rome at the time of the Gallic War. Caesar's *Commentaries* has been called the most perfect specimen of immediate history known to literature.

A training in the turning of the Latin idiom into good English introduced an important method, now so common in the teaching of this classical language, in harmony with the Report of the Classical Investigation. Dr. Francis K. Ball gave to many of the books the impress of his wide and accurate knowledge.

During the succeeding years the list of the Ginn classical books grew apace and included various editions of Cicero, Virgil, Ovid, Horace, Sallust, Catullus, Livy, Martial, Plautus, Tacitus, and others.

JAMES B. GREENOUGH   WILLIAM WATSON GOODWIN

GEORGE LYMAN KITTREDGE

In 1886 William C. Collar, principal of the Roxbury Latin School, called on Edwin Ginn with a Latin manuscript which he had named *The Beginner's Latin Book*. His manuscript, written in conjunction with M. Grant Daniell, principal of the Chauncy Hall School of Boston, consisted of the elements of Latin grammar, vocabularies, lessons, and readings. In this compact volume exceptions were for the most part eliminated, the Latin text was easy, the application was direct, and the reviews were systematic. The book had a phenomenal success throughout the land, and was a not inconsiderable factor in toning up the study of Latin in the high schools.

Many years later Benjamin L. D'Ooge, head of the Latin department of the Michigan State Normal College, brought to the house many Latin books which have had a wide sale. His *Elements of Latin* was a work of great merit in its presentation of English grammar and Latin grammar in conjunction, its interesting reading lessons, and its graphic presentation of derivatives.

It was at this juncture that the great Latin investigation was launched by a large committee of those who were distressed over the decline in the relative position of Latin in the secondary school and over the enrollment in Latin classes throughout the country. Mason D. Gray of Rochester, New York, was the executive secretary of the committee which conducted the investigation and rendered the report. The report was so thoroughgoing a piece of work and met

[33]

with so cordial a reception at the hands of the classical teachers of the country that naturally many publishers turned to Dr. Gray for a new series which would embody the recommendations for the first two years of the study of Latin. When Dr. Gray was approached by our firm, he had already before him many proposals from other publishers. After a visit to Boston, where he met Thornton Jenkins of Malden, Massachusetts, who already was known as a leading educator and a skilled textbook-writer, he concluded to throw in his lot with Ginn and Company and to collaborate with Mr. Jenkins.

The great series entitled *Latin for Today* was the result. The first book appeared in 1927. It emphasizes the reading of Latin, and abounds with stories of Roman life, religion, manners, and customs. The vocabulary and the syntax are strictly limited, but ample attention is given to the relations of Latin and English.

In the Ginn list, intended to uphold classical culture, may be found not fewer than forty-eight volumes on Latin. When Edwin Ginn announced his plan for a wide list of classical texts, Thomas Davidson wrote:

" Perhaps only those who believe with Matthew Arnold that what our modern world most needs is an infusion of that ' sweetness and light ' which made the ancient world so habitable and so fruitful in greatness, can appreciate the work you are doing, in bringing the masterpieces of classical literature, in attractive form, before the young minds of the American people."

◇

CHAPTER FIVE

THE STUDY OF GREEK AND SANSKRIT

GREEK, the sister of Latin, claimed Mr. Ginn's attention from the very beginning. Professor William Watson Goodwin of Harvard was one of the most original and accurate Greek scholars of America. He had, shortly before this time, published elsewhere a work of profound scholarship entitled *Syntax of the Greek Moods and Tenses,* a work which elicited the warmest approbation not only of the scholars in American colleges but also of the dons in Oxford and Cambridge. In the latter university it was recommended for students who were candidates for high classical honors in the Classical Tripos. The London *Athenaeum* said, on a disputed classical matter, " We would appeal to the high authority of Professor Goodwin, of Harvard, in his admirable *Syntax of the Greek Moods and Tenses.*" The New York *Nation* wrote, " After the acute investigation of German scholars, it remained for the ' practical American ' to give the clue to the protasis and apodosis."

Mr. Ginn had a peculiarly keen eye for outstanding contributions to classical knowledge, and he recognized in the author of the *Syntax of the Greek Moods and Tenses* a world authority. He went to Cambridge and asked Professor Goodwin if he would write a Greek grammar. Professor Goodwin reached into his desk, drew forth a manuscript, and said quietly, " I have already done so." In triumph Mr. Ginn returned to Boston with the manuscript, a work of remarkable conciseness and authority. It opened the door to

Greek literature and Greek thought, and was welcomed by scholars as presenting the most recent studies on accidence and syntax. Then, not being content with the grammar alone, Mr. Ginn secured from the earlier publisher the *Syntax of the Greek Moods and Tenses*, and thus placed his firm in the forefront of the classical field. These volumes, he wrote, gave him entrance into all the best schools in the United States.

Professor Goodwin died on June 16, 1912, and at the October meeting of the Massachusetts Historical Society, President Eliot read a paper on his scholarly attainments and his influence. In this paper he told the following anecdote to illustrate the veneration in which Professor Goodwin was held.

"A few years ago a committee consisting of Canadian professional and business men, charged to prepare a new constitution for the University of Toronto, visited Cambridge to inquire into the organization of Harvard University. After a long conversation with the committee in my office, I started with them from University Hall to point out some of Harvard's characteristic buildings and equipments. On our way across the college yard from University Hall to Phillips Brooks House I saluted Professor Goodwin, who was walking rapidly on the same path toward University. The gentleman with whom I was walking said to me, 'Who was that fine-looking old gentleman we just met?' I replied: 'That is Professor William W. Goodwin.' He started and exclaimed, 'Not Goodwin's

Moods and Tenses? ' ' Yes,' said I, ' the same '; whereupon he announced loudly to his comrades behind him, ' That old man with the fresh complexion and white hair is Goodwin's *Moods and Tenses* and *Greek Grammar.*' Whereat they all turned round, and took off their hats toward Professor Goodwin's back."

John Williams White had graduated at Ohio Wesleyan University, Delaware, Ohio, and was made professor of Greek at Baldwin University. He edited for Ginn and Company an edition of Sophocles' *Oedipus Tyrannus.* In this he helps the student to grasp the plan and thought of the tragedy by showing the "grand entanglements of the divine decrees, the will of the immortals, which no human force may escape or gainsay."

When Professor Goodwin saw the work, he was so impressed by its scholarship that he offered White a place in the Greek department at Harvard. White accepted the appointment, and thereafter, for a quarter of a century, the two men worked together. Their names were names to conjure with in the classical world.

White's *Greek Lessons*, intended to accompany Goodwin's *Greek Grammar*, was soon published. This was followed by his *Beginner's Greek Book*, combining in one volume the essentials of grammar, exercises, and reading lessons.

There soon followed Goodwin and White's *Anabasis* and Goodwin's *Greek Reader*. This reader went farther than other similar books of that day. It contained

[39]

selections not only from the *Anabasis* but also from the *Apology* and *Crito* of Plato, with extracts from Thucydides and Herodotus. The history of the Grecian world was opened to the student in his second year, when he met Miltiades and Cyrus. He read the trial of Socrates and the story of Xerxes sitting "on the rocky brow which looks o'er sea-born Salamis."

Other Greek books in this ambitious list were Euripides, Demosthenes, Lysias, Pindar, Aristophanes, Pausanias, and the well-known Iliad and Odyssey, edited by Professor Thomas Day Seymour of Yale, a noted scholar in the world of Greek literature. Dr. Seymour's son, Charles Seymour, the profound historian, is now president of Yale, where his father for so many years held the Hillhouse chair of Greek. In 1915 Professor John Williams White published his *Scholia on the Aves of Aristophanes*, the preparation of which he had begun in 1903 at the suggestion that scholars would welcome the publication of such part of his material as is given in that volume.

Not a little of the success of the Greek series was due to the beautiful Porson Greek type, which was used in the Ginn books. One has only to compare a page of an early Iliad with a page of Seymour's Iliad and Odyssey to see how much more attractive the latter is.

The Porson type was an outgrowth of the work of the great Attic Hellenist, Richard Porson. Toward the end of the eighteenth century he became Regius

Early Greek type

Πάτερ ἡμῶν ὁ ἐν τοῖς οὐρανοῖς·
Ἁγιασθήτω τὸ ὄνομά σου,
ἐλθάτω ἡ βασιλεία σου,   10
γενηθήτω τὸ θέλημά σου,
ὡς ἐν οὐρανῷ καὶ ἐπὶ γῆς·
Τὸν ἄρτον ἡμῶν τὸν ἐπιούσιον   11
δὸς ἡμῖν σήμερον·
καὶ ἄφες ἡμῖν τὰ ὀφειλήματα ἡμῶν,   12
ὡς καὶ ἡμεῖς ἀφήκαμεν τοῖς ὀφειλέταις ἡμῶν·
καὶ μὴ εἰσενέγκῃς ἡμᾶς εἰς πειρασμόν,   13
ἀλλὰ ῥῦσαι ἡμᾶς ἀπὸ τοῦ πονηροῦ.

The Porson Greek type

professor of Greek at Cambridge University, England,
at the early age of thirty-three.

Porson's handwriting of Greek was so perfect that
a new font was fashioned on it. For nearly three
hundred years Europe had followed the French Royal
type, fostered by King Francis the First to promote
the study of Greek in his realm.

The Porson type was adopted by Oxford and
Cambridge, the latter university using it for the first

[41]

time in 1826 for an edition of Euripides. It soon led all other fonts on the continent of Europe.

Tempora mutantur. The reign of Greek has long since passed away. It is not required for admission to any college in the land. Is the world losing something of culture and intellectual progress with the passing of the study of the Greek language? Let Macaulay answer, who, in writing of the great works of Athenian genius, says:

" From hence have sprung, directly or indirectly, all the noblest creations of the human intellect; that from hence were the vast accomplishments and the brilliant fancy of Cicero, the withering fire of Juvenal, the plastic imagination of Dante, the humour of Cervantes, the comprehension of Bacon, the wit of Butler, the supreme and universal excellence of Shakespeare. All the triumphs of truth and genius over prejudice and power, in every country and in every age, have been the triumphs of Athens. . . . Her power is indeed manifested at the bar, in the senate, in the field of battle, in the schools of philosophy. But these are not her glory. Wherever literature consoles sorrow or assuages pain, wherever it brings gladness to eyes which fail with wakefulness and tears, and ache for the dark house and the long sleep, there is exhibited, in its noblest form, the immortal influence of Athens."

Another step in the promotion of classical culture was the publication of the Harvard Oriental Series.

The *Sanskrit Grammar* of Professor William Dwight Whitney of Yale was an outstanding contribution. It carried the name of Edwin Ginn to the great universities not only in America but also in Great Britain and on the continent of Europe, and afforded an easier approach to the mother tongue of the Indo-European family of languages. Professor Edward Delavan Perry of Columbia wrote a *Sanskrit Primer*; and Professor Charles Rockwell Lanman of Harvard, earlier an outstanding pupil of Professor Whitney, wrote his inimitable *Sanskrit Reader*, based on the Nala episode in the *Mahābhārata*. Its rich notes, and its remarkable comparison of the roots that are common to the branches of the Indo-European family, have never been surpassed. That the study of classical philology was of serious moment in colleges of that day is illustrated by the sale of these books.

In his *Week on the Concord and the Merrimac*, Thoreau writes:

"While lying thus on our oars by the side of the stream, in the heat of the day, our boat held by an osier put through the staple in its prow . . . our thoughts reverted to Arabia, Persia, and Hindustan, the lands of contemplation, and dwelling-places of the ruminant nations."

He describes the Laws of Manu and refers to the philosophy of the *Bhagavad-Gītā* and of the *Hitopadēsa* and the sacred songs of the Vedas.

[43]

Thoreau took it for granted a century ago that the genius of Sanskrit literature was a part of the knowledge of the educated man and woman.

Believing that a knowledge of Anglo-Saxon is necessary for a correct knowledge of English (and one great university requires it in an English major subject), the house published an Anglo-Saxon Library, led by Carpenter's *Anglo-Saxon Grammar and Reader*, to aid in the study of the continuity of development of kindred dialects and to make a beginning in the field of classical philology. In this Library were Chaucer's *Parliament of Foules, House of Fame*, and *Troilus, Beowulf*, Cynewulf's *Christ*, and Caedmon's *Exodus* and *Daniel*. The books were published under the general editorship of Professors James W. Bright and George Lyman Kittredge. Professor Kittredge appears here for the first time on the list of authors of the house of Ginn. For forty years thereafter he took a large part in writing and editing books on English, Anglo-Saxon, and Latin, bringing to his task the real scholarship which made his courses at Harvard famous.

CHAPTER SIX

◇

PERIODICALS

THE Department of Political Science at Columbia University was particularly noted in the late eighties and thereafter for its distinguished corps of teachers, among whom were Giddings, Seligman, Burgess, and Mayo-Smith. These men, who formed part of the body that made up the Academy of Political Science, decided to publish a magazine, *The Political Science Quarterly*, for the discussion of topics of interest in economics, politics, and public law.

On Mr. Plimpton's recommendation Ginn and Company published the *Quarterly*, and for three decades it bore the Ginn colophon. The *Princeton Review*, an excellent publication, was purchased by the house and merged with the *Political Science Quarterly*.

The *Yale Review* also bore the Ginn imprint. Its editors were outstanding Yale men: George P. Fisher, George B. Adams, Henry F. Farnham, Arthur T. Hadley, and John C. Schwab. The *Review* devoted itself to articles reflecting the most advanced and scholarly thought. A few of the articles in the first number (May, 1892) will show what it aimed at doing for American scholarship. The historical scholar Edward Gaylord Bourne had an article on " The Demarcation Line of Pope Alexander VI "; Henry Villard wrote on the " German Tariff Policy," and Walker contributed " Massachusetts and the Saybrook Platform."

Later the Yale University Press became the publisher of the *Yale Review*. It is today an outstanding example of profound American scholarship.

Not content with these contributions to culture, Ginn and Company took a step to even higher realms, publishing the *Philosophical Review*. The editor was Dr. Jacob Gould Schurman, at that time dean of the Sage School of Philosophy, Cornell University.

The announcement of the *Review* might be thought to be a reproduction of an announcement in the stoa at Athens in the days of Pericles, had such a method been in vogue. In this age of mechanical development it is interesting to read that the *Review* was to cover the field of general philosophy, including, along with the older subjects of logic, metaphysics, and ethics, the newer subjects of psychology, aesthetics, pedagogy, and epistemology, both in their systematic form and in their historical development.

Some idea of the rare atmosphere in which the *Review* moved may be gained from a few of the titles in the first two numbers. Professor William James of Harvard contributed " A Plea for Psychology as a Natural Science "; Dr. Hay Calderwood of the University of Edinburgh reviewed Herbert Spencer's *Animal Ethics*; Dr. J. E. Oliver of Cornell discussed natural sciences and the philosophy of nature; Dr. Andrew Seth of Edinburgh furnished an article on " Psychology, Epistemology, and Metaphysics."

In view of the contents of magazines widely read today, it may be questioned whether Tennyson was correct in saying that the thoughts of men are widened with the process of the suns.

Other journals published by the firm were *School and College*, the *American Journal of Physiology*, the *American Naturalist*, the *Zoological Bulletin*, and the *Publications of the Dante Society*. It also published the *Transactions of the University of Pennsylvania*, *Harvard Studies in Classical Philology*, *Harvard Historical Monographs*, and the *Classical Review*. A typical number of the *Classical Review* contained articles on " The Chronology of Themistocles' Career," " Mahaffy's *Problems in Greek History*," " Notes on St. Paul's Epistles," " Stoic Philosophy," " Collations from Cicero," and a review of Leaf's *Translation of the Iliad*.

If American education failed to reach a high level, it was not the fault of Ginn and Company. Sir Philip Sidney said that a person " who shoots at the midday sun, though he be sure he shall never hit the mark, yet as sure he is he shall shoot higher than who aims but at a bush."

More than fifty years ago, as a contribution to general culture, Ginn and Company began the publication of a series of Handbooks on the History of Religions. The books were under the general editorship of Morris Jastrow, professor of Semitic languages in the University of Pennsylvania. They were designed to give an exposition of the beliefs, rites, religious art, and religious literature of particular religions, each in a separate volume. The religions treated were those of India, Babylonia, Assyria, the Ancient Teutons, Persia, Egypt, and Israel. The editors were the leading

Semitic and Indo-European scholars of the day, including Saussaye, Hopkins, Jastrow, Jackson, and Toy.

The Handbooks won the instant approval of the great philologist Max Müller. They were too expensive to be profitable to the firm, but their publication was in keeping with the spirit of the house to press ever forward the frontiers of knowledge for the schools.

In the same spirit another book was added to the list. One day a venerable clergyman called on Mr. Plimpton. He introduced himself as Father Francis Barnum, a Jesuit missionary who had spent years in work among the Innuits, beyond the Arctic Circle. He had used his leisure in studying the language of this Eskimo family, and had built up a full and scholarly grammar of their tongue. Mr. Plimpton had a love of the unusual. Here was a work that had never been done before and would perhaps never be done again. In 1901 Ginn and Company published the book in the interest of philology and as a contribution to the world's culture.

CHAPTER SEVEN

◆

MUSIC SYSTEMS

THOUGH Mr. Ginn paid full devotion to the classics, he did not overlook elementary education. Probably no other single step ever taken by him from a financial point of view was as epochal as his acquirement of the Mason Music Course.

Luther Whiting Mason was born in Turner, Maine. On account of the poverty of his people he was brought up by his stepbrother in Gardiner. Born with a keen love of music, he developed it in Boston, studying under Lowell Mason, George F. Root, and William Bradbury. He then became a teacher of music in the public schools of Gorham, Maine, in Philadelphia, and in Louisville, Kentucky. He was called to Cincinnati, where his work was of so outstanding a character that he was invited to take charge of the music department in the elementary public schools of Boston. Here he directed music in the public schools for fifteen years. The great educator John D. Philbrick of Boston spoke of him with great enthusiasm.

" Luther Whiting Mason [he said] was a teacher of large experience, an enthusiast in the work, a man of the rarest genius for teaching children, a student of pedagogy, with a spirit of self-sacrifice that constantly reminded me of the career of Pestalozzi, and thoroughly acquainted with the best things that had been thought and said and done about teaching children vocal music."

[53]

At the time of his appointment to the Boston public-school system, there was no regular method of teaching music. The instruction consisted of learning songs by rote from choral books or volumes of songs, one of which, by Lowell Mason, had at that time a fair sale.

But Luther Mason believed that music should be the heritage of every child in the schools, and that it should be taught, not in haphazard manner, but by careful progressive methods, as fully graded as the courses of study in arithmetic, the English language, or geography. In keeping with this idea, he worked out a series of books and charts unlike anything the school world had ever seen. Every grade was carefully covered, and the children, moving on from the simple rote-days of the primary grade, ascended step by step to a fuller appreciation of music and to learning to read by note. The course was strengthened by graphic charts, which developed the lesson in keeping with the pupils' books. The series was first published by Lewis B. Munroe of the New England Conservatory of Music; but apparently the inability of presenting the books properly to school authorities caused the system to be a failure.

Mr. Ginn came in contact with the plan through his chance acquaintance with Luther Mason, who explained the idea underlying the system. Realizing the great value of the plan, Mr. Ginn bought Munroe's books, and under his careful guidance the success of the series was almost instantaneous. Nearly every school authority in city and town recognized the value of this clear-cut, progressive system, and introduced it into the elementary and high schools. The method of books and charts spread from the Atlantic to the Pacific, and music became at once a part of the regular school curriculum. The financial as well as the educational success of this enterprise greatly aided Mr. Ginn in building up the general list for which he had already formed extensive plans.

In 1876, at the Centennial Exposition in Philadelphia, there was an exhibit of the house of Ginn. In walking about at the Exposition, Luther Mason came by chance to the Ginn exhibit, and happened to see a Japanese standing before the Mason charts and copying them. Mr. Mason introduced himself to the stranger, who told him that he had been sent by the Japanese Imperial government to see the exhibits, especially as they related to education. As a result of this visit, Mason was invited to go to Japan to revise the music system by introducing his music scale in place of the scale then in use. The new system spread through the empire, and for years music in Japan was known as the Mason song. Mason remained in Japan for three years. For further study he now visited Germany and was pleased to see that his system had been translated into German, a wonderful tribute from the land of song.

It has been said that the Mason Music Course did more for the cause of music in the schools of this country than any other single factor since graded education began. In the development of his course Mr. Mason was aided by two outstanding supervisors of music in Boston, Julius Eichberg and Joseph B. Sharland.

Some years later (1896) a new series called the Educational Music Course was published, and seven years later the New Educational Music Course. The new editors were James M. McLaughlin, director of music in the public schools of Boston, George A. Veazie of Chelsea, and W. W. Gilchrist of Philadelphia, a noted American composer.

Holding as it did the leading place in music in the schools of the nation, the house maintained its front rank by publishing in 1920 the Music Education Series. Under the direction of an outstanding genius in music, Elbridge W. Newton, the firm secured three of the leading musicians of the land — T. P. Giddings of Minneapolis, Will Earhart of Pittsburgh, and Ralph L. Baldwin of Hartford — to write and to launch the new series. Some idea of the intensive work required to produce a music series can be obtained by a reference to the words of Mr. Newton regarding the Music Education Series of seventeen years ago. Speaking of its three authors, he tells us that they came to Boston periodically for three years, sat in consultation with psychologists, musicians, research workers, poets, and composers, and finally evolved a superior plan for music education.

CHAPTER EIGHT

◇

THE CENTENNIAL YEAR

THE YEAR 1876 was an important one for the house, being the year of the meeting of Mr. Ginn and George A. Plimpton. Melville Dewey, who had been at Amherst College with Mr. Plimpton, was in Boston one day in July, on his way to visit Edwin Ginn, when he met Mr. Plimpton by accident and invited him to go along with him.

Mr. Ginn was so impressed with the cultured, restlessly energetic young Plimpton that he offered him a position for the summer to sell textbooks on commission in Pennsylvania. This state was chosen by Mr. Plimpton, since he wished to visit the Centennial Exposition in Philadelphia.

In the fall Mr. Plimpton entered the Harvard Law School; but the next year, instead of returning to the study of law, he became an agent for Ginn and Heath, with headquarters in New York City. In 1881 he was admitted to the firm, which now became Ginn, Heath, and Company.

Mr. Plimpton's early agency-work covered a very wide field. He made a keen study of finance, which stood him in good stead in his forty years as treasurer of Barnard College and in his relations with leading bankers and men of business. He foresaw what books were needed, and he was happy and successful in his occasional approach to authors. No pent-up Utica possessed his soul. In 1887, through his initiative, the house opened an office in London. Mr. Plimpton would have the firm produce books that would appeal to the entire English-speaking world, whether in the British Isles or in the Federated Malay States or in Australasia. As a result, Ginn and Company are the only American publishers who have maintained their own office in London to meet, with regular or special editions, the needs of the schools and colleges of the British Empire.

Mr. Plimpton also inaugurated, with Miss Evelyn West Hughan, a very successful foreign department. He was for many years a trustee of the Constantinople College for Women and of the Union Theological Seminary. He and Mrs. Plimpton were guests of honor at the sixtieth anniversary of the founding of Doshisha University in Japan, a university founded by an Amherst student, Joseph Hardy Neesima, the story of whose life outrivals fiction.

Aside from his active work in the firm, Mr. Plimpton's avocation was the gathering of more than five thousand manuscripts and books which tell the story of the growth of education from the earliest times to the present. Step by step he built up this wonderful collection. Where a gap existed, he sought out, with the greatest care, the place of the missing volume, and unless it was in the British Museum or some great public library, he never desisted until he had made it his own.

The collection, now in Columbia University, covers manuscripts before the middle of the fifteenth century, and printed books after that date, many of

GEORGE A. PLIMPTON   LEWIS PARKHURST

HENRY H. HILTON   CHARLES H. THURBER

them illustrating the ancient plan of the trivium and the quadrivium. There are manuscripts of the fourth-century Donatus, of the sixth-century Priscian, of the ninth-century Alcuin, of Ebrardus and of Boethius. There is also the first arithmetic that was printed with a date — that of Treviso, in Italy, of 1478.

Printed books of the early sixteenth century include a Greek text of Euclid, works of Melancthon and of Erasmus, as well as the sixteenth-century Latin grammar of Lily, used for decades in the great public schools of England. There is a vellum manuscript of Solenius, a Roman geographer of the third century, the first printed edition of which appeared in Venice in 1473. The Camers edition of this author, printed in 1520, contains what is, so far as known, the second engraved map of the world in which the name "America" appears. In this collection one sees a page of Donatus's grammar printed by Gutenberg before he printed his famous Bible. Here also is the largest collection of hornbooks in existence. Mr. Plimpton's interest in the venerable books of the ages led to his membership in the Mediaeval Academy of America. He loved "the best that has come to us out of the past."

His keen study of American colonial affairs is shown by his membership in the venerable American Antiquarian Society, the Massachusetts Historical Society, and the New York Genealogical and Biographical Society. His museum of Americana at his Lewis farm in Walpole is a veritable treasurehouse of the stirring days of the French and Indian Wars, in which his forebears took so active a part.

Mr. Plimpton was for thirty-two years a trustee of Phillips Exeter Academy, to which he gave the Playing Fields. For more than a quarter of a century he was a trustee of Amherst College, and for a large part of the time chairman of the board. For forty years he was treasurer of Barnard College, " whose cradle he rocked," as Dr. Butler, the president of Columbia University, said in 1929 when conferring on Mr. Plimpton the degree of Doctor of Letters.

On the death of Edwin Ginn, Mr. Plimpton became chairman of the firm, a position he held for seventeen years. In 1931 he became an inactive partner.

In recent years Mr. Plimpton was the author of two scholarly works, *The Education of Shakespeare* and *The Education of Chaucer*. These volumes are illustrated by facsimile pages of the books used in the schools in the days of these immortal writers.

Mr. Plimpton died in 1936, at the ripe age of eighty years. On his death Dr. Frank Pierrepont Graves, chancellor of the University of the State of New York, wrote of him as " America's foremost educational publisher."

One of Mr. Plimpton's teachers at Exeter was George A. Wentworth. Mr. Wentworth had been for some time at work on a geometry. He had had

[62]

a wide experience in teaching and knew the mind of the high-school and academy student. He tested the problems in the classroom and noted carefully where any unusual difficulties arose.

Wentworth presented his manuscript to Ginn and Heath. A glance at the work showed its distinguished qualities. There were at the time four geometries in wide use. In looking at the pages of the best of these, one saw at once how unattractive the work was. The theorems were explained with a plethora of words, and to follow the demonstrations and diagrams it was necessary to turn the pages constantly back and forth. Teachers well know how loath pupils are to engage in this type of exercise.

Wentworth had a new point of view. He demonstrated every theorem by the use of symbols; he put every diagram in juxtaposition with the text; he completed every theorem on its page; he differentiated clearly between hypothesis, conclusion, and proof; he supplied an abundance of problems to test the minds of the youths. The result was a book that compelled thought, the author's motto being " Learn to do by doing." It is believed that he was the first American writer to advocate the performing of original exercises by the pupils so as to make them independent and to give them confidence in themselves.

Wentworth's *Plane Geometry* swept the country, the most successful high-school textbook, Edwin Ginn declared, in half a century of textbook-publishing in America. It was, as well, the cornerstone of the great Wentworth mathematical series.

In its simplification of the subject, Wentworth's geometry led the way to the introduction of the subject into the lower grades. France and Germany in that day taught geometry to pupils ten years of age, in connection with drawing. Today the subject is presented in our grammar grades through intuitive geometry.

For many years the Regents of New York State published annually the results of an inquiry sent to all Regents' schools as to the books in use in these schools. Year after year Wentworth's geometry led by an overwhelming plurality. Indeed, its success reminds one of the occasion when the American yacht *America* won a great race in England. When Queen Victoria was told of the result, she asked, " What yacht came in second? " The courtier answered, " I am sorry to say, Your Majesty, there was no second."

The Wentworth geometry was followed in time by a complete series up to the calculus. In many forms and editions the Wentworth texts in mathematics were outstanding for many years.

The Wentworth *Primary Arithmetic* was largely the work of one of the ablest elementary teachers, Miss E. M. Reed, principal of the New Haven Training School.

In the *Grammar-School Arithmetic* published in 1890, one of the old-time arithmetics of that day, there were many important new features, among them the practical nature of the problems. Like other cumbersome features, our old friends, " the men building the wall three feet high and fifty feet long in six days, and so on," disappeared. An arithmetic of that day, and that too by a normal-school principal, gave a single example in fractions which covered one third of a page.

When objection was raised to an arithmetic loaded to the gunwales with long, tedious, involved, stupid, and useless problems, the answer for its retention in the schools was, " If the pupil mastered all the problems in the book, he would know arithmetic."

We are reminded of the cartoon of Mopey Dick and the Duke standing before the great Public Library of New York. The Duke says to Mopey, " I suppose if one read every book in that library, one would be educated."

A new feature in the Wentworth plan was the introduction of decimal fractions immediately after the fundamental processes and before common fractions, since Wentworth believed decimals presented no great problem for the child.

An interesting departure was the enlistment of Dr. Thomas Hill, who had been president of Harvard College, to work with Wentworth on a high-school arithmetic. One might easily picture a former

[65]

Harvard president working on a text on quaternions, but it was an innovation to see one at work on an arithmetic.

In the high-school arithmetic the problems recognized the existence of science by basing many of its problems on chemistry, astronomy, physics, and other branches of science, and by giving banking also an honored place.

An amusing story is told of the chapter entitled "Choice and Chance," which appeared in Wentworth's first algebra. Some objection to the chapter was made by a large Quaker school, on the ground that it might encourage pupils to gamble. Before the printing of the next edition the chapter was removed.

Wentworth was a most prolific author. Up to 1896 he had written alone or with coadjutors no fewer than forty-one texts, ranging from primary arithmetic to analytic geometry.

CHAPTER NINE

◇

AN EDITORIAL DEPARTMENT
MYERS'S HISTORIES

THE FIRST office of Ginn and Company in New York was at 4 Bond Street. To this office came in 1885 a young man, Justin H. Smith, who asked Mr. Plimpton for a position. Smith had graduated from Dartmouth in 1877 with marked scholastic achievement, and accepted a position with Scribners', where he remained until they sold their textbooks to another publishing house. He was now accepted by the firm, and took up his work in the Boston office. He was a remarkable scholar, being equally at home in the classics, history, and modern languages. His avocation was the cello.

In 1887, at the suggestion of Mr. Parkhurst, the firm established an editorial department. Mr. Smith joined with Mr. Ginn as co-editor. In the editorial department he found a multitude of activities, such as examining manuscripts, interviewing authors, selecting format and type, paper and binding, and preparing circulars and general advertising matter. He took a large part in the launching of the Montgomery Histories, the Myers Histories, and the Frye Geographies, three great successful projects of the firm. Many of the original ideas in the geographies, Mr. Frye said later, were advanced by Justin H. Smith.

In 1889 Mr. Smith was taken into the firm, and remained in the editorial department until 1898, when he resigned to accept a professorship in modern history at Dartmouth College.

From his earliest days Smith had been interested in French, particularly in old French. As a result of this interest he published in 1899 a charming and authoritative work on the troubadours of Provence, entitled *The Troubadours at Home, their Lives, their Personalities, their Songs, and their World.*

To secure a correct view of the land of the minstrels, he traveled through southern France and northern Spain, much of it afoot, taking pictures of the scenes in this region of southwestern Europe. His book was a fascinating contribution. In it the songs the troubadour thrummed on his viol, lute, or harp are rendered into faultless English rhyme. The very names are redolent of the spirit of the period: Carcassonne, Aix, Albi, Arles, Avignon, Tarascon, Orange, Vaucluse.

Before taking up his college work Mr. Smith had been invited by the firm to go to Puerto Rico and Cuba. As a result of this trip he became interested in the Spanish language and Spanish-American history. He gave up his ancient French for his new love.

In 1908, on his retirement from the Dartmouth professorship, he spent many years in the archives of Spain, Louisiana, Texas, and Mexico, gathering data for his valuable histories, entitled *The Annexation of Texas* and *The Mexican War*. Of the latter work the *Sun* of New York City said, " It need never be done again."

Professor Smith died in the midst of his researches into early American history. Thus ended the work of this gifted scholar, who had made accurate and profound contributions to Spanish-American history. Had he lived he might, perhaps, have cleared up some of the difficult problems about the Aztec, Toltec, and Mayan cultures.

On Mr. Smith's retirement from the firm (1898), Mr. Hilton, as we shall see, took the helm of the editorial department, to be followed by Dr. Charles H. Thurber.

In 1883 there were only nine agents to represent the house of Ginn in America. In 1884 W. S. Smyth became a representative for New York and Pennsylvania. Later he went to Chicago, where he took charge of the rapidly expanding business of the firm.

In 1885, after four years of the partnership of Ginn, Heath, and Company, Mr. Heath withdrew from the firm and formed a new company called D. C. Heath and Company, with headquarters in Boston. By a most amicable arrangement Mr. Heath took almost the entire modern-language list of Ginn, Heath, and Company, and many of the books on science, to start his new venture. There were two histories, however, that for a time hung in the balance: Sheldon's history and a manuscript of *Medieval and Modern History*, by Myers. Both Heath and Ginn desired the Sheldon history.

In many aspects Sheldon's history was novel. Above all else, it was modern, being designed upon the application of scientific methods to the teaching of history. It required a large amount of collateral reading, a novel feature at the time. The author, Mary D. Sheldon, was teacher of history in the Oswego (New York) State Normal School. While the question of which book should go to Ginn and which to Heath was still unsettled, George A. Plimpton took the Myers manuscript home with him and read it carefully. The next evening he went to Winchester to spend the night with Mr. Ginn. He had taken the manuscript with him, and after reading selections from it, he pleaded with Mr. Ginn until two in the morning to accept the Myers and to give the Sheldon to Mr. Heath. This plan was carried through.

On the withdrawal of Mr. Heath the firm name became Ginn and Company, which it has continued to be to this day.

Philip Van Ness Myers graduated at Williams College in 1871, and in 1879 became president of Farmers College, Ohio. Later he was for many years professor of history and political economy in the University of Cincinnati. He had written, a few years before this time, an ancient history, which had been published by Harper & Brothers, New York. It was for the general reader, and hence did not have a wide sale.

The *Medieval and Modern History*, published in 1885, was distinctly a high-school textbook. It aimed, as the author said, at dealing, not with the incidental features of the life of the race, but with its social, political, literary, and religious development, giving prominence to the virtues of mankind rather than to their vices. It told the story of civilization since the meeting, in the fifth century of our era, of Latin and Teuton upon the soil of the Roman Empire of the West. Among the outstanding scholars with whom Dr. Myers frequently conferred as he progressed with his work were Pelham of Trinity College, Oxford, Meyer of the University of Berlin, Burr of Cornell, and H. Morse Stephens of the University of California. The firm then bought the *Ancient History* from Harper & Brothers, changed it into textbook form, and reset it to correspond with the *Medieval and Modern History*.

The Myers Histories were another milestone in the development of the house of Ginn. It is probable that no textbooks of history ever written in America or elsewhere enjoyed for forty years the unbounded success of these clear, interesting textbooks, with their unusual charm of narration.

CHAPTER TEN

◇

OFFICES OF THE FIRM
FRYE'S GEOGRAPHIES

As EARLY as July, 1875, Ginn and Heath had secured offices in Tremont Place, Boston, their home for many years. Tremont Place was literally a dead-end street, leading from Beacon, the terminus being the famous Granary Burying Ground. Here were buried three signers of the Declaration of Independence : John Hancock, Samuel Adams, and Robert Treat Paine; Josiah Franklin and his wife, parents of Benjamin Franklin; James Otis and the victims of the Boston Massacre; as well as many other distinguished citizens of Massachusetts.

The windows of these offices looked over the quiet God's acre, as do those of the famous Athenaeum Library.

When the Tremont Place buildings were removed for a new business structure, the firm secured the noble Brewer house on Beacon Street, overlooking the Common. With its beautifully carved black-walnut mantels, bookshelves, and wainscoting, it was deemed to be one of the outstanding residences of the day. The Brewer house had been erected on the site of the old John Hancock residence.

It was believed that this would be the permanent office of the firm; but the growing business of the State required an enlargement of the neighboring Statehouse, when two white marble wings were added to the brick front designed by Bulfinch. The Brewer house was torn down; and the firm moved to Ashburton Place, where it still remains.

[77]

The first New York office was, as we have seen, at 4 Bond Street. It was later changed to 743 Broadway (opposite Astor Place), where Charles Scribner and Sons had their offices. Still later the firm moved to 70 Fifth Avenue, the present address.

In 1891 an office was established in Columbus.

Some years later the Chicago office was moved, under Mr. Hilton's wise direction, from the crowded Loop to Prairie Avenue, on the South Side, where the firm erected its own building, on the façade of which are to be seen the names of Froben and Aldus, the great publishers of medieval days. This part of the city has now become the center of the textbook-publishing trade.

Meanwhile, to meet the needs of the growing business in the South, offices had been established in Atlanta and Dallas, and in 1923 the San Francisco business was transferred to the firm's own present offices on Second Street.

The rapid growth now seen in the elementary business of the house was owing to the success of the Stickney Readers, the Knox-Heath Language Series, the Montgomery Histories, the Wentworth Arithmetics, and the Blaisdell Physiologies.

Blaisdell was greatly aided by the widespread enactment of laws largely under the stimulation of the Woman's Christian Temperance Union. These rather stringent laws required the teaching, in all public schools, of the deleterious effects of the use of alcohol and narcotics. For nonobservance of the law, there were rather severe penalties. This movement was the beginning of the drive of the prohibition forces, which reached its climax in 1919 in the adoption of the Eighteenth amendment to the Constitution of the United States. In 1933, this amendment was repealed.

As early as 1869 the house obtained from another publisher the first part of Hall's Our World Geographies. In 1872 it published the second part. This series received the warm endorsement of the great naturalist Louis Agassiz. Eighteen years later there occurred one of the greatest forward steps of the house, when Ginn and Company recognized in Alexis Everett Frye the apostle of a new day in the subject of geography.

Mr. Frye was born in North Haven, Maine, in 1859. His father was a deep-sea captain. The son instinctively grew to appreciate the study of land and shore forms, harbors, currents, winds, rainfall, shipping routes, and commerce.

He graduated from the English High School of Boston, and received his master's degree from Harvard College and his LL.B. from the Harvard Law School. He now moved to Quincy, Massachusetts, where he became principal of a grammar school at the time when the Quincy method was rendering somewhat famous the little city in the Old Colony.

He later became training-teacher in the Cook County Normal School of Chicago, and aroused in his students a love of geography to a remarkable degree.

Frye delivered hundreds of lectures throughout the West, and on one of his tours so impressed the school authorities of San Bernardino, California, that in 1891 he was elected superintendent of schools of that beautiful city, where on all sides orange groves fill the landscape. One of the largest of these groves was developed at Highland by Mr. Frye himself, who heartily took part in this splendid enterprise.

Under the auspices of Harvard University, Frye accompanied an expedition of geographers and scientists to Russia, where, by authority of the Czar, remarkable opportunities were given them to visit Russia as far south as the Caucasus and Georgia. Mr. Frye often told of the wonderful trip down the Volga, where, according to tradition, the boatmen are wont to sing at their work.

Frye's beginnings as an author were modest indeed. In 1888 he published a small volume entitled *The Child and Nature*, the first geography ever published with work in sand modeling. It had also a notable chapter on globe relief and comparative geography. Being an earnest student of the works of Humboldt and Ritter, Frye next published (1891) *Brooks and Brook Basins*, a type of introductory geography and reader from a new point of view. He did not limit the child to a study of mere forms of land and water, but related the study to the active agencies or forces which cover the earth with life and which

[80]

ALEXIS EVERETT FRYE

© Bachrach

WALLACE W. ATWOOD

make it a living, working, producing organism. He emphasized man's relation to the earth, and his life as affected by climate, products, and industries, now a twice-told tale, but at that time somewhat novel. Frye introduced many poems of nature from the works of the best writers for children.

The Child and Nature and *Brooks and Brook Basins* were the small seeds from which grew Frye's splendid volumes on geography; for when the editors of Ginn and Company saw these modest books (which Frye had published elsewhere), they began negotiations for a series of geographies.

Following the natural method of teaching by topics, Frye's *Primary Geography* led the way by giving the pupil an idea of the earth as a whole, thus making the globe a unit of study and making the study of this important subject a help in preparing children for life. The physical map indicated elevations in bold relief. There was no need of legends about land two thousand or six thousand feet high; for the picture told the story. To the young beginner the maps picturing the flora and fauna were a delight. Then there were special maps, in color, to show the area of leading products, such as iron, coal, wheat, corn, and cotton, drawn especially for the book by Henry Gannett of the United States Geological Survey. Thus in a primary geography the child began his work in the study of industry and commerce, even before he realized it.

Although one fourth of the human race live on delta plains, no school geography before Frye's had described these plains or told how they were formed. The illustrations were woodcuts, perhaps the last large work to use them before the woodcut era gave way to the half-tone plate, so widely used today.

The members of the firm were united in the belief that the modern geography had at last arrived, and the order for the first printing called for a hundred and ninety-six thousand copies, a greater number than had ever been printed for the first edition of a textbook.

The *Primary Geography* (1894) was soon followed by the *Complete Geography*. The series received the endorsement of the members of the Conference on Geography, appointed by the famous Committee of Ten, of the Royal Geographical Society of England, and of the Geographical Society of France.

The publication of Frye's Geographies consigned to limbo the old-type sailor geographies then in use. In less than two years eight venerable series disappeared. A special edition of Frye's *Complete Geography* was published in England and another in Canada. An edition was written for the Philippines, and one in Spanish for Spanish-American use. Frye was always pleased at the thought that young people were studying his books along the Hudson and the Tombigbee, on the banks of the Pasig, upon the highlands of Colombia, and in the quiet villages of Devon. It may be said, indeed, that their use was world-wide.

CHAPTER ELEVEN

◇

THE ATHENAEUM PRESS

THE EARLY New England agents were M. W. Hazen and Everett O. Fisk. On Hazen's retirement Fisk became for a time the general and only agent. In 1886 he retired to give his entire attention to his rapidly growing teachers' agency, which he had founded a few years before. William E. Pulsifer, superintendent of schools in Leominster, Massachusetts, took Fisk's place. He was assisted by Thomas B. Lawler, who came to the house on his graduation from Holy Cross College. Mr. Pulsifer remained in New England until he joined D. C. Heath and Company, of which corporation he later became president.

On his graduation from Bowdoin, Willian H. Greeley, who had a special interest in the make-up of books, joined the staff. A student by nature and ever a lover of books, Mr. Greeley undertook, with great enthusiasm, the study of the materials, processes, and art involved in their making, and became an outstanding builder of textbooks. For nearly fifty years he has been a vital factor in this work.

In few departments of educational publishing have greater improvements been made than in the covers of textbooks. The dull, uninteresting, repellent covers of our earlier days have given way to the bright blue, red, yellow, and green covers of the present day, with decorative lettering and artistic design on waterproof cloth in ink and stamped in gold from dies of brass.

One artist, Charles R. Capon, whose genius combines the classic with the modernistic, designs covers exclusively for the firm. Three remarkable recent illustrations of his genius are shown in the vellum *edition de luxe* of Kittredge's *Shakespeare*, Muzzey's *History of Our Country*, and Robinson, Breasted, and Smith's *Earlier Ages*.

On January 1, 1887, at the invitation of Mr. Ginn, Lewis Parkhurst joined the New England agency force. Mr. Parkhurst had been a grammar-school principal in Fitchburg, Massachusetts, and principal of the high school of Athol. At this time he was principal of the high school of Winchester, Massachusetts. In his school were two of Mr. Ginn's children.

The growing high-school and college business of New England needed the attention of a special agent. Mr. Parkhurst gave up the principalship of the high school and entered his new field. He was so successful in this work that in 1889 he became a member of the firm, devoting his time thenceforth largely to finance and to a critical undertaking on the part of the firm, namely, the establishment of the Athenaeum Press.

Charles G. Wells, who was in active service with the firm for fifty years, tells the story of the steps leading to this.

It is impossible, he says, to say when Edwin Ginn first conceived the idea of manufacturing his own publications. There is good authority, however, for

[86]

THE ATHENÆUM PRESS

the statement that in 1878, when Mr. J. Stearns Cushing left the University Press and began business for himself in Boston by starting a book-composition shop, it was with the distinct encouragement of Mr. Ginn, and, it is said, with promises of financial support. In 1881 Cushing did the composition of all the new Ginn books, the electroplating being done by H. C. Whitcomb and C. J. Peters. In 1882 Cushing moved from his original location in Boston, at Federal and Milk Streets, to 16 Hawley Street, where he remained for many years. Most of the presswork was in the hands of Wright and Potter, in Post Office Square, and Rockwell and Churchill, in Arch Street. The foreman of the pressroom of this latter concern was James S. Berwick, who soon afterward headed the firm of Berwick and Smith. The bookbinding was done chiefly by the T. Y. Crowell Company and Ephraim Adams, and the binding of pamphlets by S. K. Abbott. Practically all his book paper was purchased by Mr. Ginn from S. D. Warren and Company. Much of Mr. Ginn's success was owing to the confidence with which he was able to inspire this concern, and the consequent financial assistance and support furnished by S. D. Warren and Company. In the matter of manufacturing, there was one exception, since the single item having the largest sale, Mrs. Knox-Heath's *Language Lessons*, was for a few years manufactured under contract by a concern in New Hampshire.

It was not long after this time that Mr. Ginn thought the time had come when he could begin to do his own printing and binding. In the fall of 1886, through the assistance of George A. Plimpton, Henry A. Maley (a young New York printer) was engaged to buy machinery, install it, and set up a pressroom for Ginn and Company in Boston. Mr. Ginn had personally taken a long lease on a new building just erected at the corner of Pearl and Purchase streets, doubtless with the hope of filling this building eventually with the manufacturing activities of Ginn and Company. The pressroom was ready, and actual printing started early in 1887, with an equipment of one stop-cylinder press, two two-revolution presses, and one drum-cylinder press, though it seemed doubtful whether there would be work enough to keep these four presses occupied throughout the year. Somewhat later two Adams flat-bed presses were added to the equipment, these being considered particularly advantageous for short runs.

As for the binding, Herbert M. Plimpton in the latter part of 1882 had, with the encouragement of Ginn and Company, set up a bindery in Boston, and thereafter did most of the work of this character. Soon after Ginn's pressroom was ready, Mr. Plimpton's bindery moved to the upper floors of the building in Pearl Street. At this time his assistant was his younger brother, Howard E. Plimpton, and William J. Marsh was the general foreman. The Plimpton bindery was naturally doing work for other concerns as well as that of Ginn, and had a capacity of two thousand books a day. The rapid growth of the business soon compelled additions to the printing plant, and from time to time new and larger presses were added. In 1891 Ginn and Company purchased the bindery from Herbert M. Plimpton, taking over Howard Plimpton as superintendent; and shortly thereafter the bindery ceased to do any work but that of Ginn and Company. At this time machines for folding flat sheets and for sewing books were recent and had not come into general use, so that a considerable part of the folding and sewing was still done by hand. Books were rounded by hand, and the backing machine was worked by hand. The cutting of paper and of the edges of books and the stamping of covers were about the only other operations done by machines. Trimming machines for trimming two or more edges of books at one operation were still undeveloped. In 1892 a composition room was prepared on the second floor of the same building, under charge of Gustav Weinschenk. The Press may be said to date from this time.

In the early years of manufacturing, the head of each department had a personal financial interest in his department, which was conducted like a separate business. By 1895 the business had grown very rapidly, and many important additions to machinery and equipment had become necessary. At this time

Ginn and Company bought out the interests of the superintendents and became sole owners of the Press. It soon became evident, however, that a considerable saving in expense and a great saving in convenience, with a closer control of all our operations, would be accomplished by establishing a bookmaking plant away from the center of the city, where all our operations could be carried on with ample room for stock and shipping and with space for additional growth. Such were the reasons that led the firm to consider and finally decide upon the construction of a special building to house the Athenaeum Press.

The site selected in 1896 for the new press was in Cambridge, on the bank of the historic Charles River. The work of planning and supervising the building of the Press was given to Mr. Parkhurst.

When finished, the Press was considered to be one of the most complete printing plants in the world. The name " Athenaeum Press " was suggested by Justin H. Smith in honor of the great Athenaeum Library, under whose shadow had been the early offices of the firm. Indirectly the name recalled Athena, the goddess of wisdom, whose impressive statue, sculptured in Rome, graced for a quarter of a century the façade of the Athenaeum Press.

Later the Press was much enlarged, and was then able to produce, if necessary, forty thousand bound volumes a day. The daily handling of this vast quantity of books was for half a century under the able direction of William I. Emerson. In comparison with the meager equipment of the first pressroom in 1887, the Athenaeum Press today stands as a mighty monument to the army of the firm's loyal workers.

Mr. Parkhurst not only had a remarkably broad view of business, but in his private life he exemplified the duties of the citizen. He aided in developing the park system of his native town, and he represented his district both in the House of Representatives and in the Senate of Massachusetts. To him alone is due the credit for the building of the model prison at Norfolk, Massachusetts, a remarkably progressive step in modern penology. It is interesting to note that in the prison is a picture of Mr. Parkhurst, contributed by the prisoners themselves in recognition of his great work in freeing them from the squalid conditions of the State Prison in Charlestown. He retired from the firm in 1933, after forty-six years of active and conspicuous work. He is a life trustee of Dartmouth and received from the college the degree of Doctor of Laws. In memory of a devoted son he gave the college its administration building.

Among the many high-school books that came from the press of Ginn and Company was Lockwood's *Lessons in English*. Miss Husted (who later became Mrs. Lockwood) was a teacher of English in the high school of New Haven.

On visiting the school, Mr. Parkhurst had heard of the wonderful work in English accomplished by

Miss Husted. He visited her class, and later called on her, when she showed him the manuscript of a first-year high-school text embodying the ideas used in her teaching. Ginn and Company published the book at once; for it came at a time when the schools were beginning to take up the study of English in earnest. It is probably safe to say that at this time English was not even a requirement in the entrance examinations of most of the colleges of the country.

Mrs. Lockwood's book combined in one volume the first year and a half of study. It contained a brief history of the English language, with illustrations of its growth from other tongues, and also a thorough course in rhetoric and composition, with drill on the common errors in the use of English and with emphasis on letter-writing. Seven American authors were the basis of study, and the book was of such aid to the pupils in doing original work that it was an immediate success. Edition after edition, year after year, the pages of the book rolled from the presses. It was another landmark in the progress of the firm.

In 1891 Fred M. Ambrose was admitted to the firm. Mr. Ambrose had for some years been an agent of wide experience with the J. B. Lippincott Company, the distinguished and venerable Philadelphia publishers. His headquarters were in New York. Mr. Ambrose remained in the firm until 1915, when he had to retire on account of ill health.

CHAPTER TWELVE

◇

THE ERA OF THE TRUSTS

IN THE late eighties the American nation was swept by a movement to form single corporations out of former actively competing businesses. Railroads, steel industries, steamship lines, oil companies, food-producers, and manufacturers, all were drawn into the vortex. Small houses, fearful of their very existence, were in haste to join, lest they be crushed in a war at once ruthless and conscienceless.

American Big Business had suddenly come to believe that only in monopoly and restraint of trade could its business be successful. To these great combinations was popularly given the name of " trusts," a misnomer if ever there was one.

It was not long before the movement spread to the educational publishing field. At this time the house of Ginn and Company was, in volume of business, the sixth in the nation. Above it, so to speak, were five large houses, each with a long list of books, especially for elementary and grammar schools, and a staff of highly trained executives and agents. These five houses, actively competing, controlled 90 per cent of the common-school business in geographies, American histories, arithmetics, language lessons, spellers, and writing-books. In high schools they did not have more than 30 per cent of the business.

In 1890 action was taken to combine the big five, and eventually about thirty houses, large and small, were absorbed under one direction.

One organization was now apparently dominant in the educational field, following in the steps of big business everywhere in the land. It was a critical time for the house of Ginn and Company. The firm was invited to join the combination, an act which meant the end of the house as an entity. To refuse would perhaps place the firm in the path of a juggernaut.

Mr. Ginn and his partners (for the house has always retained the partnership form) did not falter for a moment in their decision, though they recognized the possible untoward conditions that might and probably would confront them.

The partners declined to join the new combination. Mr. Ginn wrote that American teachers would never recognize monopoly; that they would always demand the best textbooks, in a free field; that there could be no monopoly of brains; that any day some outstanding teacher might produce a new book which would render obsolete, almost overnight, all existing texts on that subject. The correctness of Mr. Ginn's reading of the future was soon proved by the course of events.

CHAPTER THIRTEEN

◇

ENLARGEMENT OF THE FIRM

IN 1889 the firm was fortunate in securing for its high-school and college business Osmyn P. Conant, whose name is still held in loving remembrance by the older generation of educators of New York State.

Mr. Conant was born in Massachusetts. He graduated at Dartmouth College, and on leaving college taught for a time in Bermuda. He was so loved by his pupils that in later days many of them wrote to him asking him to be godfather, *in absentia*, for their newborn babes. To each he sent a silver gold-lined cup suitably engraved. Natality would appear to have been frequent; for we have happy memories of seeing Osmyn P. Conant sauntering forth to Tiffany's with great frequency.

On returning from Bermuda, Mr. Conant taught in Torrington, Connecticut, and later became head of the school system at St. Albans, Vermont, a position he held when he joined Ginn and Company. He brought to the house a remarkable ability. Not only was he a thorough classical scholar, but he knew both French and Spanish and he kept pace with the latest researches in science. To the high schools and colleges that he visited he brought not only a knowledge of his books but a remarkable grasp of the important educational problems of the day. The textbook business has never known a more cultured gentleman. He was admitted to the firm in 1892. He died in 1910.

In the minutes of the firm on his death, we read:

" In the turmoil of a sharply competitive business, he was never even tempted to be ungenerous or unkindly. The business banner which he so long upheld was as unstained as Bayard's knightly banner."

The growth of the business in the Central Atlantic States brought about the opening of an office in Philadelphia. In this field the active agent was Ralph L. Hayes, whose special interest was the high school and the college.

Mr. Hayes graduated at the University of Vermont. After a period of teaching he entered the house to look after its interests in Pennsylvania, Maryland, and the District of Columbia.

Mr. Hayes was a careful student, with a character of stanch reliability. To the day of his death he never failed to hold the friends he made in his visits through his extensive field. On the same day in 1892 that Mr. Conant became a partner, Mr. Hayes was admitted to the firm.

After eight years of service, ill health caused him to retire. Some years later, having to some extent regained his health, he re-entered the agency field of the house with the assignment of a limited area, which he himself selected. This he covered until his death.

In the meantime the common-school branch of the house had been rapidly growing. The success of the Knox-Heath language lessons, the Stickney Readers,

(STANDING) T. P. BALLARD, G. A. PLIMPTON, R. L. HAYES, L. PARKHURST, O. P. CONANT, J. H. SMITH, S. S. WHITE

(SEATED) F. M. AMBROSE, T. W. GILSON, E. GINN, F. B. GINN, H. H. HILTON

and, above all, the Montgomery American Histories required the house to enlarge its agency work in this field.

In the late eighties there was an active campaign in Vermont, where each of the fourteen counties was required, under a new law, to make a free-textbook adoption. Mr. Parkhurst was sent to take part in the campaign.

After a careful study of the situation he returned to Boston. He told Mr. Ginn that if he wished to build up a successful common-school business he needed many skillful agents. His advice was that he ought to begin by engaging two agents whom he himself had recently met in Vermont and who, to put it mildly, had swept the field. These men were at the time working for William Ware and Company, publishers of the Franklin arithmetic and readers. One of the authors of the Franklin arithmetic was Edwin P. Seaver, superintendent of public schools in the city of Boston.

Mr. Ginn acted at once on Mr. Parkhurst's suggestion. One of the men was Selim S. White and the other was Austin H. Kenerson. Both were graduates of Dartmouth. With his charm of personality and warm spirit of camaraderie, White became one of the most successful managers the textbook business has ever known. His work often took him far afield, for he had charge of the work in many of the Southern States, as well as in New England.

In 1891 he was admitted to the firm; but, unhappily for the house and the schools, he died nine years later.

The second man whom Mr. Parkhurst had recommended was Austin H. Kenerson, a native of Vermont. Kenerson graduated from Dartmouth in 1876. After experience in teaching, he became associated with William Ware and Company.

Like Mr. White, Mr. Kenerson had great ability as an agent. He made a careful study not only of his books but of the school problems of the day. He came to the firm in 1893, at a most auspicious time. Far and wide in New England he introduced in towns and cities the Montgomery Histories and the Frye Geographies, and assisted Miss Cyr in the preparation of the upper books of her successful series of readers.

In 1900 he was admitted to the firm. Five years later he was suddenly called to the great beyond. He was always welcomed by school authorities and is still remembered by the older generation of educators,

"Against whose names not yet
The fatal asterisk of death is set."

An alcove in the Baker Library at Dartmouth perpetuates his memory.

CHAPTER FOURTEEN

◇

THE MONTGOMERY HISTORIES

MR. GINN had remarked, as we have seen, at the time of the formation of the text-book combination, that no monopoly in any educational subject could count on permanency, since at any time a new book might appear which would change the whole situation almost overnight. In 1890, for example, there were six American histories in active use in the schools, one of which had an unusually wide sale. Now suddenly Montgomery's *Leading Facts of American History* appeared. A few years before, Montgomery had published with the firm a small volume which he called *Leading Facts of English History*. It was a skeleton history. Two years after publication it was entirely rewritten, in enlarged form. Mr. Montgomery had a style of great charm. His text was vivid, interesting, and particularly helpful to the pupil through the summaries at the end of the chapters, the studies of social problems, the interesting footnotes and questions, and the full bibliography. The illustrations were woodcuts and many of the maps were in color.

The book was an immediate success. In hundreds of high schools and preparatory schools it became the standard English history, and so remained until changing curricula eliminated English history, as a special subject, from the schools.

Soon after its publication the reports of the history's success began to flow in from all parts of the country. One day Mr. Montgomery appeared in Mr. Ginn's office. Mr. Ginn congratulated him on his success, and then said quietly, "Mr. Montgomery, you don't think you could write for us an American history, do you?" Mr. Montgomery's simple answer was, "I should like to try it." Without further ado he set actively to work, and soon his *Leading Facts of American History* appeared.

This book was another forward step in the history of the firm. It changed, almost in the twinkling of an eye, the position of the house in the elementary schools and gave it a position which two years before was undreamed of. The book had a vivid style, like the narrative of an eyewitness, and within fifteen months there were printed two hundred and ninety-five thousand copies.

In selecting the leading facts from the mass before him, Montgomery used rare judgment. He presented the causes and results graphically, especially with a view to the industrial, commercial, and social development of the people. His summaries rounded up the chapters, and his footnotes were intensely interesting.

The style and charm of the book held the pupils. Two illustrations of this direct appeal might be noted. In referring to John Cabot, Montgomery writes:

"Henry VII was notoriously fond of money, and knew how to hold on to it; but in this particular case he tried to be generous. He appears to have given

John Cabot a small pension; for after his death the following memorandum was found in the king's private expense book: ' *10th August, 1497.* To him that found the new isle, £10.' "

The king certainly got his money's worth; for on that voyage of Cabot's the English based their claim to North America.

In treating Maryland at the time of the establishment of the Protectorate in England, Montgomery tells of the organization of a new Maryland Assembly, which " declared that Lord Baltimore no longer had any rights whatever in the colony which he himself had founded, and to which he had invited many of the very people who now turned against him. That action must have reminded him of the story of the camel that begged shelter in his master's tent, and when he got it, kicked the owner out."

To Montgomery's grammar-school text was soon added a volume for elementary schools. He wrote a high-school history to meet the needs of the changed courses of study, which had begun to require American history in the fourth year of the high school in place of the history of England.

Civics had not yet begun to have a place in the schools. To meet a growing need in this important subject, Jesse Macy, professor of history and political science in Iowa College, wrote for the house a text-book which he named *Our Government*, a book which galvanized into life what had been a dull subject.

◇

CHAPTER FIFTEEN

THE WINNING OF THE WEST

To meet the wide extension of the business west of the Alleghenies, Ginn and Company increased the membership of the firm. In 1891, to promote the business in the rich States of Ohio, Kentucky, West Virginia, and Tennessee, the firm established an office in Columbus, under the direction of Thomas P. Ballard, who had been an active agent in this field. Ballard graduated from Amherst in the class of 1876. In 1890 he became a partner, and was later transferred to Chicago. W. S. Smyth, who managed the Chicago field for many years, left in 1893 to become an executive of D. C. Heath and Company. Ballard retired in 1897.

In 1893 T. W. Gilson, who for many years had been with Lippincott, left that company to enter the house of Ginn. He became a partner and was associated with the Chicago office. This territory, entrusted to Mr. Gilson for the special promotion of elementary books, was almost an empire. It covered the entire West, all the Southwest except Texas, and, with the exception of California, the States of the Pacific coast.

The problems facing Gilson as a directing partner in this vast area were manifold indeed. There were state adoptions, city adoptions, as well as the usual small-town adoptions. Gilson was ever present on the firing line, taking part in many of the leading contests.

He brought to his work a wise and inspiring leadership which, together with a kindly sympathy with

[111]

the many agents under him, made him one of the most popular members of the firm during his long service of over twenty years. As a result of his active direction and that of his partner, Henry Hoyt Hilton, who had gone out to the Chicago office, the Chicago territory, extending from Ohio on the east to the Pacific coast (excepting only the State of California), soon produced 40 per cent of the entire business of the firm.

In 1890 Dartmouth College had conferred on Henry Hoyt Hilton the degree of Bachelor of Arts. Hilton was born in classic Cambridge, but had lived in Lowell, where he attended the grade schools and the high school. On graduation from college he became an agent for Ginn and Company, covering the New England States. Besides his New England activities, he took part in textbook campaigns in Ohio, where he met the keenest competition on the part of one of the members of the combination, which would willingly brook no competition in a field claimed as its own.

In the reorganization of the Chicago office Hilton joined Ballard and Gilson. He was admitted to the firm in 1894. At this time there were only ten agents in the entire West. Mr. Hilton, who was an indefatigable worker, traveled far and wide in the great states that made up the Chicago territory, being especially active in high-school and college work. Some idea of the active growth of high schools in the

Western field may be seen from St. Louis. When Mr. Hilton first visited the city, there was but one high school; today there are over thirteen times as many.

Hilton was always on the watch for possible authors, and many of the outstanding men on the Ginn list came to the house through his activities and his keen judgment.

Later he was elected a trustee of Dartmouth, and gave to the college its golf fields.

In the World War, Hilton had direction of the work of the Students' Army Training Corps, covering seven hundred colleges of the country, and adjusted the claims arising from the work of the corps. He is a trustee of Colby College. For twenty years he has been trustee and treasurer of the Chicago Congregational Seminary, to which he has given a beautiful chapel in memory of his son.

When Justin H. Smith retired, Hilton was asked by the firm to return to Boston. He spent two years in the editorial chair, and then went again to the Chicago office, to the active life of the blossoming and progressive West, continuing his active interest in the editorial department by harmonious co-operation with his successor and friend, Dr. Charles H. Thurber, of whose great work we shall speak later.

When the question of the code for the textbook publishing business under the National Industrial Recovery Act was brought up at a meeting representing a hundred and fifty publishers, it was a marked tribute to Mr. Hilton and to the firm that he was elected by acclamation as the permanent chairman of the code committee.

In 1919 he was delegated to close the London office. After studying the situation he urged its retention with greater activity. Robert D. Morss, an American, was given charge. The business was incorporated as an English house, under the name " Ginn and Company, Ltd., London." Not only were American books pushed by the house, but a progressive step was taken in the publication of texts written by leading British educators and published in London.

In 1931, after Mr. Plimpton became inactive, Hilton was elected chairman of the firm. To this position he has brought an experience gained through years of active participation in business and in every phase of educational publishing, and has unified the activities of Ginn and Company into a well-knit, national organization.

He has received the degree of Doctor of Laws from Northwestern University, Colby, and Dartmouth.

The marvelous growth of the high-school and college business in the Chicago area brought about the need of assistance to Mr. Hilton, who from 1905 to 1909 had had sole charge of the Chicago office. Dana W. Hall was selected as Mr. Hilton's assistant. Hall was educated at Colby College, of which institution he later became a trustee. To his work for the firm he brought a broad classical culture. He watched carefully the trend of education in the high schools and colleges of the land. At meetings of the firm one could tell from Hall's careful reports, to a fraction of a degree, the growth or decrease of the study of Latin, general science, or any other subject in the schools of the central West. He knew thoroughly not only his own texts but also those of his competitors. He was able to recommend, after careful analysis, the books that should be published for the immediate future, as well as what books already published needed to be revised, even if they were still enjoying a wide sale. In this difficult and foreseeing estimate he was particularly proficient.

In 1909 he was admitted to the firm. He died in 1926.

CHAPTER SIXTEEN

❖

THE MODERN-LANGUAGE QUESTION

WHEN Mr. Heath withdrew from the firm of Ginn, Heath, and Company to form a new publishing house, he took as a part of his interest a large share of the firm's foreign-language list. Ginn and Company therefore had to build up again an almost entirely new department.

Mr. Ginn believed that French could be taught with success even in the primary grades, and as early as 1886 he induced Sophie Doriot to write a French book for children, which was made attractive with bright illustrations.

The idea did not have a wide acceptance, however. Modern languages, contrary to the custom abroad, were not introduced into American schools until the first year of the high school. Apparently the extensive use of French in Europe, and among large numbers of well-educated persons elsewhere, led to its introduction into the curriculum of many of our high schools. German was also taught *pari passu*, especially in the great states of the Middle West. The teaching of Spanish in the early days was almost negligible in spite of the fact that it was the universal language of the millions of Mexico, the Caribbean countries, and South America except Brazil. The Spanish war of 1898 and the rising tide of Imperialism (under the euphemism of " manifest destiny "), which brought ancient and storied lands (outside our borders) under the American flag, led to the wider teaching of Spanish. The thoughts of the American people at that time turned toward the tropics and Spanish America.

The World War had, of course, decided repercussions in the schools, and German was dropped very generally throughout the country. Spanish gained during this period and in the years of readjustment, but German again returned to the curricula as the echoes of war died away.

Led by the very successful *Elementary French* of Aldrich, Foster, and Roulé, and the *Première Année de français* of Bovée, hundreds of French books covering stories, songs, games, plays, and histories furnished the texts called for in the high schools and colleges of the land.

In German a beginning was made by the publication of Collar's *Eysenbach*. Mr. Collar, the author of the Latin books bearing his name, was a versatile scholar. On a visit to Germany he learned of a text written by Eysenbach which was enjoying a wide use in German schools for its practical presentation of the German language in the form of combined grammar, lessons, and readings. Collar adapted the book to the needs and usages of American schools. It had a wide sale.

The progress of the study of German is illustrated in modern books such as Allen and Phillipson's *First German Grammar*, Chiles and Wiehr's *First Book in German*, and Howe's *Fundamentals of German*. Müller and Wenckebach, teachers at Wellesley College, wrote

[120]

a German reader with the happy title *Glückauf*, the salutation with which miners descending into a mine or ascending from it greet one another. The pupil in this little book descends into the rich mine of German literature with stories, poems, myths, and sagas. In all, forty texts give the pupil a view of the beautiful literature of Germany, with its school life, city-and-town activities, lyric poems, comedy, the Black Forest, Saxony, Bavaria, and the Danube. Dürer, Goethe, Lessing, and Schiller speak from the pages of these books.

As early as 1880 Professor Whitney of Yale had called the attention of his publishers to the excellent work in Spanish done by Professor William I. Knapp of Yale. Knapp enlivened his classwork by a constant presentation of the manner in which the Spanish language grew, especially from Latin, Arabic, and Greek, and he showed how for centuries the four hundred years of active Roman occupation of the Iberian Peninsula had laid the basis for the Spanish language and Spanish mores.

Knapp did not content himself with the brief statement that *ser* and *estar* are the two verbs in Spanish for " to be." He showed how *ser*, indicating what is inherently permanent, is derived from the Latin *sedere* (" to sit "), whereas *estar*, signifying an incidental or temporary condition, is derived from the Latin *stare* (" to stand "), prothetic *e* being prefixed to the Latin root.

As an example of his incidental references he presented the common Spanish word *hidalgo*. The derivation of this word is generally given as *hijo de algo*, " a son of somebody," which is not convincing, since every male, Spanish or otherwise, is a son of somebody. Knapp showed that this word came from the Latin word *Italicum* (meaning " one who has the right of Roman citizenship "). Any person holding this right rose, of course, above his fellows. The Spanish word *hidalgo* is a corruption of the Latin word *Italicum*. Ginn and Company welcomed the opportunity to publish as early as 1882 Knapp's *Spanish Grammar* and *Spanish Readings*.

In 1917 appeared the first work of Carolina Marcial Dorado. This was a high-school reader entitled *España Pintoresca*. Miss Marcial is a native of the famous Spanish city Toledo, high above the yellow Tagus. She was educated in Madrid and at Wellesley. She taught in the University of Puerto Rico and at Bryn Mawr College, and is now associate professor of Spanish in Barnard College. From her pen have come to the firm many Spanish books for the elementary grades.

A First Spanish Grammar is the work of Professors Marden and Tarr of Princeton. Another *Spanish Grammar* is from the pen of Professor Coester of Stanford University. *The Essentials of Spanish Grammar* is the work of House and Mapes of the State University of Iowa.

◇

CHAPTER SEVENTEEN

AFTERMATH
OF THE SPANISH WAR

AT THE close of the Spanish-American War, Puerto Rico and the Philippines passed, as everybody knows, under our flag, and Cuba came under our temporary protection.

In keeping with the usual keen interest of the American people in education, it was decided to reestablish in these countries the school system which had been destroyed or interrupted by the war.

President Eliot of Harvard was asked by Elihu Root, Secretary of War, to recommend two educators to develop in Cuba and the Philippines a school system somewhat after the manner of those in the United States. For Cuba, President Eliot named Alexis Everett Frye, whose work in geography he had followed with the keenest interest.

In October, 1899, Mr. Frye became the first superintendent of elementary education in Cuba. He opened hundreds of schools throughout the island, drew up a complete course of study, and appointed scores of division superintendents and hundreds of teachers. Fortunately there was no problem in the matter of language, such as arose in the Philippine Islands, since the beautiful Castilian tongue was in use everywhere in Cuba.

Ginn and Company, on their part, sent Mr. Lawler to Cuba, where he remained until there had been prepared under his direction Spanish textbooks of the most modern type in elementary geography, arithmetic, algebra, geometry, hygiene, and reading.

Soon there might be seen, every morning, Cuban children trooping by thousands to the public and private schools, like their fellow students in the United States.

In developing his work Frye was greatly aided by the strong and helpful co-operation of General John R. Brooke, governor general of the island, who joined whole-heartedly with Mr. Frye by giving him without stint any governmental aid needed for the new school system. There had been, of course, many schools in Cuba before American occupation, but they were for the most part private schools. The new plan was designed to reach all the children of the island, especially those of the worker classes.

Of the hundreds of Cuban teachers, few had received any normal training, and fewer still had ever been outside the island. On the other hand, Americans had scarcely ever visited Cuba. The grim specter of " yellow jack " was at the time a powerful deterrent; in fact, life-insurance companies of that day required a policyholder to take out a special permit if he was to visit the tropics.

Believing that a somewhat broader background would greatly improve the teaching force under him, Frye devised a plan as novel as it was daring. He would transport, free of charge, thirteen hundred Cuban teachers to Harvard University for a six weeks' course in pedagogy and English. He would also give these teachers a view of the United States by moving them en masse to Chicago, Philadelphia, New York, and other cities.

In a letter to President Eliot, Frye outlined the plan. The success of the scheme required the co-operation of Harvard for the instruction and of the War Department of the United States for transport service, and financial aid from the American public to the amount of $100,000. All this was to be worked out under the direction of Harvard University.

Shortly after Frye's letter reached President Eliot, Frye received an answer by cable. It was laconic to a degree, for it contained only the single word Yes.

The face of Helen of Sparta (the poet tells us) launched a thousand ships to war against Troy. The cable of President Eliot launched three transports, with thirteen hundred teachers, for education and close, harmonious relations between the United States and the " Queen of the Antilles."

The expedition was an unbounded success. The transports reached Boston, courses of instruction were given for six weeks, and the teachers visited American cities. They returned home without the illness of a single person, or, as Frye jocularly remarked, without the loss of a single piece of baggage.

The Cuban people have never forgotten the great work done by Frye for the education of their children. Mr. Frye died on the first of July, 1936. A few days later the following message from Havana was received at Washington. Translated, it reads:

Habana
July 8, 1936

His Excellency
  Cordell Hull,
    Secretary of State, Washington.
  *I express to you in the name of the Government
of Cuba our profound condolence on the death of the
eminent educator, Alexis E. Frye, whom Cuba re-
members gratefully on account of his magnificent
work as first superintendent organizer of the primary schools of Cuba during the years 1899
and 1900.*

JOSÉ MANUEL CORTINA,
Secretary of State

July 14, 1936

His Excellency
  José Manuel Cortina,
    Secretary of State, Habana, Cuba.
  *Please accept my sincere thanks for your message
of July 8 wherein you convey the condolence of the
Government of Cuba on the lamentable death of
Dr. Alexis Everett Frye. The kindly sentiments
expressed by Your Excellency are deeply appreciated by this Government. I am sending a copy
of Your Excellency's message to the widow, who
I am sure will derive a measure of comfort from
the tribute paid therein to the memory of her
husband.*

CORDELL HULL

July 14, 1936

My dear Mrs. Frye,

    It is with deep regret that I have learned of the death of your distinguished husband, Dr. Alexis Everett Frye. The steady strengthening of the traditional friendship between the Cuban and the American people is in no small measure due to the impetus given to this cause by the effective labor of your late husband at a critical time in history. Please accept my expression of sincere condolence offered personally as well as in the name of our Government.

    That your late husband's memory is cherished equally in Cuba as in his own country is manifest from the telegram which I have received from the Secretary of State of Cuba, and of which I am sending you a copy. A copy of my reply is likewise enclosed.

                    Sincerely yours,

    (Signed)   CORDELL HULL

CHAPTER EIGHTEEN

◇

THE PHILIPPINE ISLANDS

THE SECOND problem of education before the War Department was that of the Philippine Islands. Immediately after the close of the war with Spain, the military commandant in Manila asked the Reverend William D. McKinnon, a chaplain in the United States army, to gather together the children of officers and officials, to draw up a plan for instruction, and to open schools pending the establishment of a regular system of education under the Military Commission.

To carry out the plan for a widespread school system, the Secretary of War asked President Eliot to name a director of education for the entire Philippine group. He recommended Dr. Fred W. Atkinson, principal of the high school, Springfield, Massachusetts.

Dr. Atkinson, who was remarkably well-equipped for the task, was appointed. He had received normal training, and knew the problems of elementary schools. He was a graduate of Harvard, and after studying in several German universities, as well as at the Sorbonne, he had received the degree of Doctor of Philosophy at Leipzig.

His work in the Philippines was heroic indeed. The war had disrupted the school system except for university work. The Dominican University of Santo Tomás was still flourishing, as it had been for two hundred and eighty-eight years. A college under the direction of the Society of Jesus was also in full vigor.

Dr. Atkinson divided the entire archipelago into districts, over which were placed superintendents. A normal school with progressive methods was established, in addition to the high schools. The city schools of Manila, the largest unit in the group, were directed by Dr. David P. Barrows, who came from the Normal School of San Diego, California. Hundreds of teachers were brought on transports from the United States. A full supply of the most modern American textbooks was given to the schools, with the necessary laboratory equipment. An organic act was proposed for the whole system.

At the outset the most serious of the immediate problems was the question of what language should be used in the school system. In Manila, Cebú, and Iloilo — the three most important cities of the archipelago — the language in general use was Spanish. Throughout the Islands the educated spoke not only Spanish but often French as well. In the provinces the natives spoke the local dialects of the Tagalog, Visayan, and Moro families. It required a week's active discussion for the Civil Commission to enact the organic law, one provision of which was the use of the English language as the medium of instruction in the Islands.

The Filipinos learned English very rapidly indeed, more rapidly, so far as colloquial English is concerned, than one would expect. As an illustration a story is told of a discussion on the matter of tolls. Over the Pasig River is a suspension bridge on which was levied a toll of three cents. American soldiers, and soon all Americans, paid no attention to the tolls. One day an American whose complexion had been considerably browned in military hikes by exposure to the tropical sun started across, when he heard the tollkeeper call out "Three cents." Going back to the keeper, the American carefully explained that since the United States occupation no tolls had been paid by Americans. "But you no American," replied the tollkeeper. "What makes you think I am not an American?" asked the United States citizen. "Because you no say, 'Aw, go to hell!'"

Having finished his work in Cuba, Mr. Lawler went to look into the educational situation at Manila. He arrived a few months after Dr. Atkinson had begun his superintendency. When he presented, so to speak, his credentials to Governor General Taft, the governor said, "Please extend my compliments to Ginn and Company on their enterprise in having a representative here before even the enactment of the fundamental school law."

After three years of brilliant service Dr. Atkinson resigned. His quiet dignity, strong administration, grasp of education, and human sympathy had won for him the esteem of the Philippine people.

After a short interregnum Dr. David P. Barrows, who had received the degree of Doctor of Philosophy in anthropology from the University of Chicago, became director of education.

After a time he resigned as superintendent of the city schools of Manila to take charge of the Bureau of Non-Christian Tribes, a work which gave him an opportunity to exercise his early love of anthropology in a study of the manners and customs of these primitive peoples. He soon returned to the department of education as director and nobody could have brought to the position a more complete background. He carried on and enlarged the work planned by Dr. Atkinson. He developed trade schools, founded an agricultural college, and fostered industries to build up among the people a better and fuller life.

Dr. Barrows desired to know at firsthand every condition in the Islands. To study those conditions, he traveled far and wide on horseback, by canoe, by carromata, and by rail. Since no regular method of communication existed between most of the Islands, the government on one occasion furnished him with a steamer to visit the far-flung islands of the archipelago.

For this extensive trip he invited Mr. Lawler, Ginn and Company's representative, to accompany him to study the essential needs of the Islands from the point of view of special educational Philippine texts written in English.

The trip through the archipelago was a wonderful revelation, not only of the beauties of nature but also of the cultural stage of the people. The hundreds of islands were fringed with stately coconut palms. Dense

[136]

forests on the hills in the background rose to the horizon, tier after tier. Here and there were the picturesque bamboo houses, built five feet above the ground and all thatched with nipa roofs. Fishing nets were drying along the shore, and weirs were to be seen in every shallow stream and estuary.

Occasionally a dugout with outrigger and lateen sail drifted slowly along in the gentle breeze. The sunrises and sunsets glowed with brilliantly changing colors, as if (as Edward Everett said of a similar scene) "hands of angels, hidden from mortal eyes, shifted the scenery of the heavens."

The trip extended to the great island of Mindanao. Although the Philippine Islands had a fair supply of excellent American textbooks, yet nothing in the way of special texts had been published for them. The point of view of the American textbook was naturally North American, with the United States as the point of departure. The temperate zone was, of course, in the mind of the American author. Our arithmetics were based on feet, acres, gallons, bushels, and miles. The snow scenes were fascinating, but difficult for a pupil in the tropics to comprehend.

The Filipino child had a different point of view. His world was tropical. He had never seen snow or a sled or an apple tree or a heated house or a fur coat. In weights and measures the metric system and some local measures and weights dominated his life.

To meet these conditions, Ginn and Company prepared for the Philippines a set of special textbooks based on local conditions, in as excellent a format as the Athenaeum Press could produce. The books included an arithmetic, an English grammar, language lessons, a Philippine geography, a Philippine history, a complete set of readers, and books on drawing.

Those books which met general tropical conditions were adopted by other warm countries also.

Later Camilo Osías, of the National University of the Philippines, wrote a series of modern readers for the Islands. Geographies by Hugo Miller, based on the Philippine point of view, presented a graphic picture, never before attainable, of the economic conditions of the Islands of the West (*las Islas del Poniente*), as the early Spaniards called them.

Miller was appointed Ginn and Company's representative in the Philippine archipelago, where today, with marked success, he carries on the work of the firm.

In advancing the interests of the firm in the Orient, even as late as 1905 one met experiences that showed how static in many ways (such as transportation) the Chinese were, after five thousand years of culture and intellectual advance.

On one of his early trips to China, Mr. Lawler was invited to visit the University of Soochow. Being in Shanghai at the time, he sought the best means of getting to Soochow, and learned that it would be necessary to take a canal boat up the Grand Canal.

He cut from a catalogue the name of the university with its equivalent in Chinese characters. This, it might be remarked, was not a mere translation of the name of the university, but the title given to it in Chinese, which was, in fact, an entirely different designation.

Sending a telegram to the university, Mr. Lawler went to the quay and was surprised to see a long line of canal boats. He was given a cubby-hole down in the hold, reached by a ladder. There was no heat, although it was a cold day in March. The cabin had merely a wooden bench. There was a flickering oil lamp on the wall. On the roof above the cabin were huddled scores of Chinese exposed to the chilling wintry blasts. What Chinese coolies and their families endure with patience is beyond belief.

All night long the canal boats, drawn by a small steam tug, moved slowly forward. Early the next morning Mr. Lawler arrived outside the ancient walls of Soochow, and the boats were moored along a mud bank. To his surprise, there was no one to meet him. Since he knew that Soochow was a city of great size and that the streets, like those of all Chinese cities of that day, were no doubt narrow, dark lanes, he realized how important it was not to get lost in the maze of a city where no English was spoken.

Mr. Lawler, seeing a mandarin being carried along in a sedan chair, saluted him and showed him his precious little bit of paper. The mandarin seemed puzzled for a time; but, calling one of his bearers, he sent him through the gate, and soon the bearer returned with a chair and three coolies.

The mandarin explained to them, no doubt, the object of the search. He then courteously saluted, handed back the bit of paper, and went on his way. The bearers plunged into the crowded city. It was raining, and the narrow, gloomy streets were at their worst. The bearers did not seem to know "what it was all about." Every little while they would come for the paper, go into a shop, and hold long discourse "about it and about." They would then resume their turnings and twistings, with a repetition of the visit to a shop.

After two hours, to Mr. Lawler's great relief, they came into the open; and far across vacant fields, on which were scattered ruins of apparently a not far-distant past, appeared a tower, without question an Occidental one. It proved to be the tower of the university. The ruins in the vacant fields were all that was left to remind one of the great Taiping Rebellion.

Mr. Lawler was soon before the warm, hospitable fireplace in the university. The telegram had, in fact, never been delivered.

In view of its establishments in the United States, London, and Manila, a recent widely distributed weekly said of the house that upon its offices the sun never sets.

CHAPTER NINETEEN

◇

THE TEACHING OF ENGLISH

STRANGE as it may seem, it was observed a few decades ago that the study of English in the schools did not appear to be a vital question.

Mr. Ginn had always taken a keen interest in literature as we have seen in his publication of the Classics for Children. It was his policy to secure as authors prominent leaders in this field of education.

In 1877 he wished to have an English grammar. At that time there were many grammars in use in the schools, but none by a distinguished master of the English tongue. In Yale University the professor of English was William Dwight Whitney, the ablest philologist in the Western world. His Sanskrit grammar has ever been the acknowledged authority on the ancient Indo-European language.

Professor Whitney was asked to undertake the writing of an English grammar for the house, and after much deliberation he gave his consent.

When the manuscript was nearing completion, the following incident occurred. Mr. Plimpton visited Professor Whitney and asked him how his forthcoming book differed from those in use. Professor Whitney replied that he did not know. A trifle surprised, Mr. Plimpton asked, " Have you written the book without examining other grammars? " " Of course," replied Professor Whitney. Mr. Plimpton further asked, " How do you know, then, Professor, that the work has not already been done," and, with a smile, " perhaps better than you have done it? " Professor

Whitney replied, also with a smile, " Mr. Plimpton, I examine the English of the boys that enter Yale, and if such a book had been written, the examinations would show it."

The *New York Sun*, which specialized in English under the great Dana, said of the book that it was the best English grammar ever published. Francis J. Child, professor of English at Harvard, wrote:

" I do not know that I have ever before seen an English Grammar which I would permit my children to look into, so great has been the chance that they would learn nothing, or be taught something false. I regard Professor Whitney's undertaking of the book as a service to humanity, as well as to education."

Later, as is well known, Dr. Whitney supervised the making of the great Century Dictionary and Cyclopedia. This work was a noteworthy contribution to profound scholarship and, throughout the world, marked Dr. Whitney as the leading American scholar in philology and its allied branches, a field up to this time largely pre-empted by German professors.

As early as 1879 Mrs. N. L. Knox-Heath wrote a two-book language series.

A novel feature for the time was the publication of a manual to show teachers what to do, and how to do it, by presenting plans for developing each lesson. A preliminary chapter was an outstanding contribution, for that day, of the principles of education and the art and laws of questioning as developed by

Pestalozzi. A superintendent of a large city system in New York State called the manual " a normal school in itself."

In 1900 appeared The Mother Tongue language series. The authors were Professor George Lyman Kittredge and Miss Sarah L. Arnold. This inductive series embodied the authority of a distinguished professor of English at Harvard and the rich experience of Miss Arnold, director of primary education in the public schools of Boston. It was built on the cumulative plan of emphasizing the essentials of the subject.

In 1916 there appeared a series entitled Oral and Written English, which became one of the outstanding successes of the house. The series was prepared by Harry Jewett Jeschke, who had been a teacher of English in the Central High School of Cleveland, with the collaboration of Dr. Milton C. Potter, superintendent of the Milwaukee schools, and Harry O. Gillet, principal of the Elementary School, the University of Chicago.

Another forward step in the elementary-English list was taken in 1934 with the publication of the Daily-Life Language Series, written by distinguished authorities in English: Dr. R. L. Lyman, formerly professor of the teaching of English in the University of Chicago; Roy Ivan Johnson, a specialist on functional grammar and composition and director of skills and techniques in Stephens College, Columbia, Missouri; Frances R. Dearborn, associate in education in

[145]

Johns Hopkins University; Mata V. Bear, assistant in the Division of Tests and Measurements in the St. Louis public schools; and A. Laura McGregor, a specialist in English in the progressive public schools of Rochester, New York.

With the far-reaching views of this group in making use of the reports of the National Council of Teachers of English, the series was planned to cover the work in English from the second grade through the junior high school. The manuscript was tested for six years in the classroom. The series correlates the social activities, projects, and experiences of the daily life of the pupil.

CHAPTER TWENTY

◆

NEW MEMBERS IN THE FIRM

IN THE YEAR 1893 Richard S. Thomas became a Ginn agent, with headquarters in New York. In addition to receiving the degree of Bachelor of Arts from Yale, Mr. Thomas had taken his degree in law; but instead of entering the legal profession he became associated with the University Publishing Company. In his work in New England he had met Selim White and Austin Kenerson of Ginn and Company, who were at once attracted to him. A short time later he accepted a position with the firm.

Thomas rose quickly to a commanding position in the educational field. His early work was with the New York City public-school system, in which he took the leading part in agency work.

Few men had a clearer mind for grasping vital principles. His education was so thorough that he divined the worth of a proposition instantly, but never appeared to accept it without mature reflection. His quiet dignity, reserved bearing, and unfailing courtesy won him a legion of friends who cherished his companionship. After six years of agency work he became a member of the firm in 1898. His untimely death in 1923 left a void which casts its shadow down the years.

In 1900 Dr. Charles H. Thurber took the editorial chair. Dr. Thurber graduated at Cornell University, and for a time remained at Cornell in administrative work and as instructor. He visited Europe, where he carried on his study of psychology and greatly enlarged his background of European history. He taught at Colgate, was dean of Morgan Park Academy, and served on the faculty of the University of Chicago. He received the Doctorate in Philosophy at Clark University, where he later became president of the board of trustees.

Dr. Thurber came to the house with a particularly rich background; indeed, it is impossible to imagine a richer one for the arduous work of building up the list of elementary, high-school, college, and technical books. He had the unusual experience of having taught every grade from the primary to the graduate work of the university. His early editorial work, which began with a country newspaper, covered magazines, an encyclopedia, and the direction of a list of high-school textbooks for another publisher.

The work of an editor of an educational publishing house is varied and all-embracing indeed, and Dr. Thurber was to the manner born. Whether authors talked of précis writing or of polar co-ordinates, pragmatic sanctions, gymnosperms, or vertebrate zoology, he understood the language they were speaking, even if he did not profess to be proficient in these varied sciences. During his long, active editorship many thousands of manuscripts were received and critically examined with almost unerring judgment. He separated the wheat from the chaff: those manuscripts adaptable to existing (or soon to be existing)

AUSTIN H. KENERSON   RICHARD S. THOMAS

THOMAS B. LAWLER

conditions, and those which, although worthy in themselves, did not appear to meet the immediate needs of the schools.

He created an *entente cordiale* between authors and the firm. His office radiated an atmosphere of kindliest co-operation. In 1904 he was admitted to the firm. It is safe to say that no house in the world ever published in three decades such a list of epoch-making textbooks as Ginn and Company did during Dr. Thurber's fruitful thirty-three years of editorship.

Two years after Dr. Thurber's admission to the firm, Thomas B. Lawler became a partner. From his Alma Mater he had received the degree of Master of Arts, and in 1910 that of Doctor of Laws. On coming to the house after his graduation from college he had, at the outset, as a special charge, the general agency work in the Catholic schools and colleges, which had already begun their marvelous development, until today there is an enrollment of two and a half million pupils in schools and colleges under Catholic direction. Mr. Lawler had also wide experience in agency work in public schools in all parts of the country.

When, as an aftermath of the Spanish-American War, the United States began the development of an educational system in our newly acquired territories of Cuba, the Philippines, and Puerto Rico, Mr. Lawler was called by the firm to visit our new possessions for the purpose of supervising the publication

[151]

of textbooks in Spanish for the recently acquired territories and Spanish-America and of aiding in the development of the foreign business. To carry out these plans, he visited all parts of the world, including, as we have seen, Cuba and the Philippines.

On his return from the latter islands he was asked to go to Puerto Rico. Here a new school system was being established. In 1902 Dr. Samuel McCune Lindsay was appointed Commissioner of Education. Dr. Lindsay had been professor of sociology in the University of Pennsylvania, having received the degree of Doctor of Philosophy from the University of Halle. He was a born administrator, and under his direction the new system was soon in full flower.

Ginn and Company prepared here also special texts to meet the needs of the new system as applied to the Caribbean area and South America.

CHAPTER TWENTY-ONE

◇

A WIDE MATHEMATICS PROGRAM

THE DEATH of George A. Wentworth left a great void in the list of Ginn and Company's distinguished authors. Fortunately, as happens now and then, a worthy successor, Dr. David Eugene Smith, was at hand to carry on the work in "the oldest of all the sciences."

Dr. Smith graduated at Syracuse University, from which he received the degree of Doctor of Philosophy also. He was admitted to the bar and practiced law for three years. He then became teacher of mathematics in the Cortland State Normal School, and later professor of mathematics in the Michigan State Normal College. In 1898 he was appointed principal of the Brockport State Normal School. After three years he was called to Teachers College, Columbia University, where for twenty-five years he filled a brilliant role in the chair of mathematics, retiring as professor emeritus.

The first work of Dr. Smith published by Ginn and Company was *Plane and Solid Geometry*, written in conjunction with Dr. Wooster Woodruff Beaman. It was published in 1895 and was followed in 1897 by *Higher Arithmetic* and in 1900 by the *Elements of Algebra*, by the same authors.

In all his work Dr. Smith's interest in the historical side of mathematics is manifest. Through tables of etymologies he shows how various geometric terms have risen.

Taking up the mantle of Wentworth, Dr. Smith entered upon his distinguished career as a writer of

[155]

mathematical textbooks. He was co-author of the Wentworth-Smith Arithmetics. Dr. Smith put inspiration into the work. As a result, with the publication of his *Number Stories of Long Ago* the dull arithmetic era had passed away. The child, at the very beginning of his working with numbers, enters the happy realms of Number Land, where he learns how little people counted thousands of years ago. He sees Ching by the Yellow River of China, learning from his father how to make figures on a palm leaf with brush and paint; Lugal by the Euphrates, pressing numbers on clay tablets; Ahmes in the temples of Egypt, figuring on papyrus; and Hippias under the shadow of the Parthenon, writing Greek numerals on parchment. What a happy and interesting world was opened to the child!

From time to time there appeared from the pen of Dr. Smith, in rapid succession, works on algebra, geometry, trigonometry, analytic geometry, and high-school mathematics.

Now and then he varied his strenuous programs by publishing special mathematical texts for agriculture, forestry, mechanics, commerce, and elementary science. He issued works in Spanish for the schools of Spanish-America. Three of his texts were published in China; and, in the Sultanate of Iraq, students of Bagdad vary their work by changing from the reading of the *Thousand and One Nights* to the study of Dr. Smith's mathematics in Arabic. In addition he wrote books on the teaching of arithmetic, algebra, and geometry. With Professor William D. Reeve of Columbia University and Edward Longworth Morss, he wrote the wonderfully popular *Exercises and Tests in Algebra* and *Exercises and Tests in Plane Geometry*. He also prepared teachers' manuals, keys, and other aids to teaching, ad infinitum.

In his early work he co-operated with George Wentworth, son of the distinguished teacher at Exeter, with Mullins, Karpinski, and Siceloff of Columbia, with Foberg of Pennsylvania, with Brown of Pelham, with Schlauch of the High School of Commerce of New York City, and with Harper of the Murray Hill Vocational School of New York City.

In a trip to Persia, Dr. Smith may not have seen a wilderness nor, perhaps, a jug of wine, but the atmosphere of Omar Khayyám inspired him to edit a new translation of the *Rubáiyát* of the immortal poet, philosopher, and mathematician of ancient Iran.

Dr. Smith was decorated with the Gold Star of the Order of Elmi by the Persian government, which goes to show that poetry appeals to some governments of the world.

One of the most prolific authors of mathematics that this country or probably any other country has ever known is Dr. Smith, the author or part author of no less than a hundred and forty-two textbooks, extending over the entire gamut of the science of numbers. Even as early as 1898 his reputation as a profound student of the pedagogy of mathematics was known in Germany, where Dr. Rudolf Knilling wrote an article for a German magazine, under the title "Dr. David Eugen Smith, ein hervorragender amerikanischer Rechenmethodiker."

As a contribution to world culture the firm published Dr. Smith's two volumes entitled *Rara Arithmetica*, a book of reference known in every library of importance in the world. It gives a history of the arithmetics printed before the year 1601, and is based largely on more than three hundred arithmetics in the library of the late George A. Plimpton, the largest collection of early arithmetics ever gathered by one man.

In Dr. Smith's list of twelve hundred books is the first dated practical arithmetic ever printed, the famous Treviso arithmetic of 1478. In these volumes we meet with such names as Isidore, the distinguished Bishop of Seville, Boethius, Cassiodorus, Capella, Archimedes, Euclid, the Venerable Bede, Sacrobosco, Melancthon, and many others of equal note.

Ginn and Company also published Dr. Smith's *History of Mathematics*, which contains a wealth of information on the growth of this science, not only for chronological periods but by racial contributions. Written by an outstanding authority, the work is an important contribution to human knowledge.

In two trips round the world, and in wide travels during forty years, in which he has crossed the

GEORGE A. WENTWORTH   DAVID EUGENE SMITH

HAROLD RUGG

Atlantic eighty times, Dr. Smith brought together some of the instruments used by the nations in their study of numbers, as well as a vast collection of portraits of distinguished mathematicians, all of which he has given to Columbia University. The collection numbers nearly three thousand items, relating to nine hundred and eighty-one persons.

It is interesting to note how some of these worthies rank in the hall of fame, if we are to judge by the number of portraits available. Newton, of course, leads the list with one hundred and eighty-six; then follow Descartes with eighty-nine, Pascal with eighty, Galileo with fifty-five, Voltaire with fifty, Leibnitz with thirty-seven, and Euler with twenty-eight.

Among the hundreds of instruments gathered by Dr. Smith are armillary spheres from Jaipur; celestial spheres from Nagasaki; astrolabes from India, Arabia, and Italy; sundials from Bavaria, Bohemia, Italy, and the Tirol; terra-cotta signs of the zodiac from Alexandria; a telescope from London; quadrants from Austria; compasses from ancient Rome, France, and Germany; weights from Italy; steelyards from Malabar, China, and Germany; sector compasses from England; gauger's scales from Wales; clocks from Japan; the abacus from Russia, Arabia, and China; tally sticks from England; slide rules from France; hornbooks from America; Buddhist rosaries from Mandalay. All these are but a few of the treasures gathered by Dr. Smith.

[159]

One of the most interesting series published by the house in mathematics is the Alpha Individual Arithmetics, worked out by the staff of the Summit Country Day School of Cincinnati. In each of these sixteen books, one for each half year in the eight-year course, there is within one cover a textbook, a workbook, and a testbook. The series covers the work from the first step in numbers through intuitive geometry, graphs, measurements, algebraic equations, and finance and investment. Years of preparation, and years of testing in the classroom, make this series one of the outstanding contributions to the teaching of arithmetic during the last decade. It was a successful attempt to meet the growing demand in the field of the workbook without the need of special volumes for this type of activity.

In 1937 there appeared the first of a noteworthy series entitled Daily-Life Arithmetics. The authors are Professor William A. Brownell of Duke University and Professors Guy T. Buswell and Lenore John of the University of Chicago, leaders in the field of arithmetic through their researches and experimentation, with the assistance of teachers in training.

In 1929 Ginn and Company added to their list an algebra called *Algebra for Today*, by William Betz. Mr. Betz graduated at the University of Rochester, where he received the degrees of Bachelor of Arts and Master of Arts. He joined the teaching staff of the East High School of Rochester, where he later became vice principal and head of the department of mathematics. He also taught in the Lincoln School of Columbia University, and was lecturer on education in the University of Rochester. For many years he was a member of the summer faculty of Teachers College, Columbia University. He was elected to the important position of president of the National Council of the Teachers of Mathematics, and became an adviser of the College Entrance Examination Board. In simple words Mr. Betz gives the reason for studying algebra. He says:

"Algebra has contributed the machinery for expressing in a universal language the important relationships which have become the backbone of science, engineering, and industry. In particular, the three great tools which algebra has furnished for this purpose are the formula, the equation, and the graph."

Algebra for Today was not the work of a moment; it was the result of ten years' experimentation in the classroom, where pupils of all degrees of ability were thoroughly tested. Its unit chapters, its summary of specific objectives, its emphasis on the fuller meaning of the subject and on the functional aspects of algebra, all bring out the idea that mathematics is in reality one of the major needs of the human race.

This book radiates the spirit of the classroom, and has had a very large share in saving algebra for the high-school curriculum, at a time when the subject seemed to be losing ground under a heavy barrage from the progressive group of teachers.

Welchons and Krickenberger, two outstanding teachers in the Arsenal Technical High School of Indianapolis, wrote *Plane and Solid Geometry*, which not only covers the ideas of the past but anticipates the problems of the future. Practically every possible proof of the theorems is presented until the pupil reaches the solution. This volume makes a generous use of pictures, such as bridges for the study of triangles, skyscrapers for the use of proportional lines, landscape gardening, commercial designs, drawings from the Pueblos and other primitive peoples, and even the spider's web, snow crystals, and honeycombs.

In his series of Junior Mathematics for Today, Betz shows why mathematics forms so important a part in the curriculum of the junior high school, by being the common heritage of man. These books make the subject more attractive to the pupils. How the subject fits into everyday life is shown by its wealth of illustrations, its graphs, diagrams, maps, and decorative line-drawings. It calls into action not only mathematics, but the homely subjects of food, clothing, and shelter in their vital relationship to human life.

Another remarkable course in mathematics is the Hawkes, Luby, and Touton series of algebras and geometries. In preparing this course three eminent educators took part. Dr. Herbert E. Hawkes is professor of mathematics in Columbia University and also dean of Columbia College. He graduated at Yale, where he later received the degree of Doctor of

Philosophy. In mathematical writings he has covered a wide field. William A. Luby is the practical teacher, the head of mathematics in the University of Kansas City. Frank C. Touton, until his recent untimely death, was vice president and professor of education in the University of Southern California.

In this series the mathematical treatment is complete; in addition there are historical notes telling the pupil the story of the men who in the last three thousand years have made pronounced contributions to algebra, including Vieta, Archimedes, Wallis, and many others. Perhaps no better illustration can be furnished of the point of view of the firm than their securing for this series the conjunction of the broadest scholarship, the most searching test by daily teaching, and the psychology of the child mind through the study of education.

The Dunn, Allen, Goldthwaite, and Potter *Useful Mathematics* is an illustration of the attempt to meet the diverse needs of the schools. It covers the ninth and tenth grades, and has in special view the aiding of two groups of pupils: the slower divisions and those who, taking mathematics for a terminal course, do not expect to carry on the study beyond the tenth grade. Accuracy, understanding, and happiness in the work make even the slow student (the authors believe) better fitted to meet the demands of modern life.

The Ginn list of mathematics is a roll of great teachers and great mathematicians who have shaped

[163]

and are shaping today the teaching of the subject in our schools.

From its very beginning it will be seen, therefore, that the house has contributed greatly to the promotion of mathematical science, believing with Mr. Betz that

". . . even a moderate acquaintance with the origin and the spirit of mathematics serves to bring out the fact that this great science has a universal background. It is anchored in the very nature of things. It is as indestructible as the force of gravitation and as permanent as hunger, being coextensive with nature, science, and technology. Hence the language of mathematics is part of the language of humanity. It is understood everywhere because the world is incurably mathematical. . . .

"It is absolutely true that mathematics is a universally available and indispensable servant of all mankind. In co-operation with other sciences and technology, it builds our cities, our roads, bridges, tunnels, factories, and industrial plants. It constructs our engines, automobiles, steamships, and airplanes. It makes possible the countless inventions and conveniences that have served to make modern life less arduous, such as labor-saving devices in the home, in the shop, and on the farm. It has given us the radio, the movies, and the electrified home, and it is about to perfect television. If ever our understanding of economics and our social planning are to rise above the rule-of-thumb stage and above the level of unintelligent self-interest, it will be done with the aid of mathematical principles."

CHAPTER TWENTY-TWO

◇

THE NEW HISTORY MOVEMENT

ALTHOUGH Myers's Histories were still enjoying unusual success, the house realized that a new day was dawning in history and that the curricula in the subject were rapidly changing.

During Mr. Hilton's occupancy of the editorial chair he had been successful in securing the consent of Dr. James Harvey Robinson to head a wide program in history. This program was fully carried out by Dr. Thurber. Dr. Robinson was the outstanding leader in this new movement. At this time he had already published (in collaboration with H. W. Rolfe) a volume on *Petrarch, the First Modern Scholar and Man of Letters*, a charming work on the laurel-crowned poet of Italy and Provence, the protagonist of the Renaissance.

Dr. Robinson graduated at Harvard and received his degree of Doctor of Philosophy at Freiburg, Germany. He lectured at the University of Pennsylvania, and in 1892 became associated with Columbia University, where for the next quarter of a century he was a pre-eminent leader in the newer concepts in the teaching of history. He has been called the philosopher of progress.

Dr. Robinson believed that history for the schools would be vastly improved by putting greater emphasis on matters of vital interest and by eliminating half the irrelevant and trivial material. The grateful space that might be cleared (he wrote) " by the expulsion of ninth-rate royal relatives and hundreds of minor skirmishes over long-forgotten issues could be used to

[167]

elaborate events of first-rate importance and to describe the work of a few men of supreme significance for the world: Gregory the Great, Charlemagne, Saint Bernard, Abélard, Saint Francis, Aquinas, Petrarch, Erasmus, Voltaire, Bismarck."

In 1903 he wrote for Ginn and Company his *Introduction to the History of Western Europe*, an epoch-making work that at once arrested the attention of scholars and teachers by its broad concept of history; its omission of isolated, uncorrelated facts; and its wide sweep of subjects, comprising those customs, institutions, and achievements of western Europe which embrace the true activities of man in building up modern civilization. The text, based largely on the study of primary sources, at once took its place as the leading synthesis of the era of medieval and modern history. In his preface Dr. Robinson gives a brief résumé of his views.

The student of history, he writes, "wishes to know how people lived; what were their institutions, their occupations, interests, and achievements; how business was transacted in the Middle Ages, almost without the aid of money; how, later, commerce increased and industry grew up; what a great part the Christian Church played in society; how the monks lived and what they did for mankind. In short, the object of an introduction to medieval and modern European history is the description of the most significant achievements of Western civilization during the past fifteen hundred years and the explanation of how the Roman

PHILIP VAN NESS MYERS   JAMES HARVEY ROBINSON

DAVID SAVILLE MUZZEY   JAMES HENRY BREASTED

Empire of the West and the wild and unknown districts inhabited by the German races have become the Europe about which we read in the morning newspaper."

Not only was Dr. Robinson among the first of historians to recommend strongly the reading of source material, but he himself supplied the material in translations. The pupil who reads of Charlemagne's personality in the vivid and intimate picture given by his personal secretary Eginhard can obtain a truer conception of the great ruler and his times than by the usual general observations about him.

Here, in the Venerable Bede's own narrative, the pupil learns of the conversion of England. From Apollinaris Sidonius he gets a view of the Saxon pirates. He can read the actual edict of the Roman Emperor Galerius, establishing Christian toleration, and in the *Anglo-Saxon Chronicle* he sees the development of modern languages.

This story of events at firsthand gives the pupil the opportunity of forming an independent judgment. Dr. Robinson would not have mankind enslaved by its past; rather he would bring the past to man's liberation.

Robinson's *Introduction to the History of Western Europe* was followed by his *Medieval and Modern Times*.

To obtain the fuller presentation of modern history required by modern courses of study, Dr. Charles A. Beard was asked to co-operate with Dr. Robinson.

Dr. Beard graduated at De Pauw University and received the degree of Doctor of Philosophy at Columbia, where for ten years he occupied the chair of politics, establishing for himself an international reputation. In 1907 Robinson and Beard produced *The Development of Modern Europe*, which pointed out how the trends of the Middle Ages passed into those of today. The book traces the development of modern thought as well as the social and governmental institutions. It presents to us the scientific and literary achievements of the later Middle Ages.

For the earlier history, before the decline of the Roman Empire, Dr. James H. Breasted was invited to prepare a text that should begin with the time when the curtain of history first rose on the blossoming civilization of the Nile valley and along the Tigris and Euphrates rivers.

Dr. Breasted, America's most famous Egyptologist and Orientalist, was director of the Oriental Institute of the University of Chicago, and led many expeditions to Egypt and the lands of the vanished empires of Assyria and Babylonia. During these years his scholarly pen contributed volume after volume on Egypt and the countries of the Near East.

In co-operation with Dr. Robinson, he wrote in 1914 the *Outline of European History*. In 1916 appeared Breasted's *Ancient Times: A History of the Early World*, and in 1935 his revision of *Ancient Times*. This book, in the judgment of many, has never in the history of textbook publishing been surpassed in beauty of format and binding, accuracy and profound scholarship, adaptability to the student mind, and exquisite and graphic illustrations.

In spite of the obstacles resulting from the World War, says Breasted, the progress made in the study of the ancient world has been one of the most remarkable advances in the history of humanistic research.

In this new book (as the preface tells us) we see the evidence of the life of man in the earliest Stone Age in northwestern Africa and in the Near East, showing the development of civilization in that period entirely round the basin of the Mediterranean, instead of merely in Europe.

We have in the book, as showing recent discoveries and researches, the story of the magnificent sculptured stairways of Persepolis, the development of Etruscan civilization in Anatolia, the decipherment of Hittite hieroglyphic inscriptions, the discovery of the tomb of Tutenkhamon, an event (says Breasted) which has perhaps done more to interest a large public in the story of the human past than any other single discovery in the history of archaeological research.

As a result of all these investigations in the Near East, the earliest edition of *Ancient Times* had to be entirely rewritten, thereby giving the publishers an opportunity of presenting it in a format worthy of the noble subject. Breasted's *Ancient Times* ended with the fall of the Western Empire.

[171]

The exacting demands of newer school curricula and history sequences require a book which covers the eras from prehistoric man through the absolute reign of Louis XIV, at times to the founding of our republic. An attractive new book, *Earlier Ages*, published in 1937, covers the story of Western civilization. It was written in co-operation by the two distinguished historians Breasted and Robinson, assisted by the research students Smith and Ware. It is essentially a textbook. Its bibliography, as well as its record of events, is of yesterday; it recognizes the advance of the social sciences, provides a preface and a foreword, and presents reviews and questions, adventures in learning, full consideration of the sources, all being part of the combined efforts of historians and teachers.

To carry on the work from the point where *Earlier Ages* ends, Professors Beard and Robinson, with the assistance of Dr. Donnal V. Smith, have written the inspiring book *Our Own Age*. In these two volumes the student has a broad view of human progress from the dawn of history to the present day. Here is a picture of man's progress in mental development, in industry, in commerce, in inventions, in science, in the arts, in religious beliefs, in literature, in the devastating periods of war, and in the more fruitful years of peace, the elements that have brought about our present civilization.

In Dr. Thurber's program appeared the name of David S. Muzzey, professor of American history at

Columbia University. Dr. Muzzey was born in Lexington, where the name of one of his ancestors may be seen on the stone that marks the early battle of the Revolution. He graduated at Harvard and received the degree of Doctor of Philosophy at Columbia.

Dr. Muzzey had a wide background. He taught mathematics in Constantinople College, by the side of the world-renowned Bosporus. Later he taught Latin and Greek in New York City. He then became professor of American history in Barnard and Columbia.

In 1911 appeared *An American History*, his first book for the house. His vigor, his accuracy of statement, his charm, and his clarity and simplicity of expression, made an immediate appeal to teachers, and his textbook was recognized at once as the foremost high-school American history.

His recent work, *A History of Our Country*, with its admirable format, distinguished typography, modern maps, and illustrations by artists specializing in history, marks the wonderful advance in textbook-making in the last quarter of a century. Dr. Muzzey's broad point of view and his impartial treatment of controversial issues places him in the forefront of American textbook-writers.

A History of Our Country may be called the standard American history of its kind. It was selected by the American Institute of Graphic Arts, among its Fifty Books of 1936, for excellence of typography and design, the only high-school textbook to be so honored.

CHAPTER TWENTY-THREE

◇

THE EXPANDING HISTORY LIST

IN THE year 1932 Ginn and Company strengthened its list in a remarkable way by the publication of the Pahlow Histories. Dr. Edwin W. Pahlow brought to his work a wide experience. He graduated at the University of Wisconsin and later received the degree of Doctor of Philosophy at Harvard. After teaching at the University of Wisconsin, at Princeton, and at Lawrenceville, he became professor of the teaching of history at Ohio State University.

Having an interesting and graphic style, Dr. Pahlow gives to his writings a magic touch. He enjoys an original point of view. His excellent text and time-charts, covering the past five thousand years, tell the pupil how the present came to be what it is. Pahlow is successful in making the history of the progress of mankind a fascinating story and in making historical characters interesting persons. He called his first book *Man's Great Adventure*. In this work he strives to make the pupil feel that he is a citizen of the world as well as of his native land, and that he needs to feel at home in both.

Pahlow seeks to increase the interest of the pupils by presenting his material in a simple and attractive style and by occasionally giving them a topic on which to write a simple exercise. For example, he asked them to write an epitaph for the grave of Socrates. One pupil drew a picture of a tombstone and wrote on it as follows: "Here lies Socrates. He tried to make the people think, and so they killed him."

Man's Achievement is a two-volume series, expanded from *Man's Great Adventure*. The first volume, *To the Age of Steam*, opens with the story of the Great Pyramid and closes with the French Revolution. The second volume, *The Age of Science and Democracy*, leads the pupil to the events of yesterday.

Pahlow's pictures are not mere embellishments. For example, the victorious gladiator in the Roman Colosseum, standing with his defeated rival beneath his foot, looks up to the Vestal Virgins to learn whether he is to give the coup de grâce or spare his fallen rival. Thumbs down tell the fatal story for the victim on the sand.

As a suitable title for the picture, Pahlow has written beneath it the following lines: " The Cultivated Roman's Idea of a Good Time. Here is a poser for those who say ' You can't change human nature.' "

Unlike most histories, these books present the story of the teeming millions of the Far East, where today there are problems that might well upset the self-sufficiency of the Occident.

It is not kings or emperors, knights or ladies, who fill these pages, but in larger measure the progress of man in art, culture, and science, to the life of today, with its machines so efficient that by pulling a lever or pushing a button anyone may have at his command labor equal to that of a hundred slaves and, as a result, the opportunity to enjoy, in everyday life, refinements and pleasures such as no monarch of old ever dared to dream of.

In his *Making of the Modern Mind*, John Herman Randall, Jr., also emphasizes this thought when he writes:

" It is literally true that for the ordinary man the main facts of human toil and enjoyment did not change appreciably from the days of Cheops, the pyramid-builder, to those of Washington, and that in the interval from Washington to our own time the transformation has been little short of miraculous. More rapid social changes now take place, in a single decade, than in whole centuries in the past; and the rate is being accelerated."

The student who reads Pahlow cannot fail to grasp the significance of these words.

As a part of Dr. Thurber's history program, Dr. Edward P. Cheyney, professor of European history in the University of Pennsylvania, was asked in 1904 to write a short history of England, a subject to which he had given particular study, as shown by his two scholarly works on the social history of England.

Dr. Cheyney's *Short History of England* is not merely the story of Plantagenet kings or queens or Tudor kings or queens; it presents a larger view of the early institutions, literary history, land conditions, manners, customs, and social life of the English people.

In 1933 the house presented to the schools *The American Nation*, written by Dr. Richard J. Purcell.

Dr. Purcell received his degree of Doctor of Philosophy from Yale University, and at present is professor of American history in the Catholic University of America. His history puts emphasis on the social and economic factors in our national life, and on the contributions made by all the elements, both racial and religious, which had a part in the upbuilding of our nation.

To bring to a focus the historical information of the pupil and to reinforce the value of the textbook, the house has published the map-exercise books in history by Bishop, Willard, Robinson, and Walker. These books cover a wide field of history, with maps, map-tracing paper, time-charts, and suggestive questions, thereby enabling the child to learn for himself how much or how little history he has assimilated. Another book to which teachers and progressive students have turned for years is Channing, Hart, and Turner's *Guide to the Study and Reading of American History*. These three noted historians have epitomized, in a single volume, the outstanding references to American history, a work of untold labor.

While the work in history has been pushed in the high schools, the colleges have not been overlooked. Dr. Muzzey wrote in two volumes *The United States of America* for college students, with emphasis on the ideals of democracy. With Professor John A. Krout of Columbia he wrote *American History for Colleges*. Professor Ross W. Collins of the University of Alberta wrote *A History of Medieval Civilization in Europe*; Professor Franklin Charles Palm of the University of California and Dr. Frederick E. Graham of San Jose State Teachers College were the authors of *Europe since Napoleon*; Professor G. Nye Steiger of Simmons College wrote *A History of the Far East*, a graphic picture of events in the vast world from Siberia to the Indies, from the third millennium B.C. to the present day. Professor Nicholas P. Vlachos of Temple University, in his *Hellas and Hellenism*, brings before the college student a picture of the culture of Hellenistic civilization. Professor Asa Earl Martin of Pennsylvania State College has written a *History of the United States*, in which, ranging from the earliest times to the present, the college youth learns of the social, economic, governmental, and cultural influences which have shaped our destiny. Professor James C. Malin of the University of Kansas shows in *The United States after the World War* the trend of present events. Dr. Robinson brought out two new volumes by revising his *Introduction to the History of Western Europe*. In the first volume, *The Background of Modern History*, he covers the period from the decline of Rome to the " Sun Monarch " of France; in the second, *Emergence of Existing Conditions and Ways of Thinking*, he shows how modern European civilization has encompassed the world.

In 1937 there appeared for colleges a new *History of England and the British Empire*, written by two Princeton professors, Dr. Walter Phelps Hall and Dr. Robert

[181]

Greenhalgh Albion. The book covers a wide sweep, dealing not only with England from Anglo-Saxon days but also with the entire British Empire to the present era. It emphasizes the constitutional phase; but it also presents politics and economics, the personalities of the Empire, and the leading place that English literature has long held.

The ever-increasing importance of Spanish-America is presented in *The People and Politics of Latin America*, written by Professor Mary Wilhelmine Williams of Goucher College. The book is a study of the national history of the Central and South American republics. Dr. Herbert Eugene Bolton has written for the house the *History of the Americas*. It presents the Western Hemisphere as a unified study. Dr. Bolton is professor of history and director of the Bancroft Library, the University of California. Under the direction of Dr. Bolton, whose exact scholarship is equaled by his deep appreciation of the early activities and achievements of Spanish officials and ecclesiastics, especially in the Southwest of our present nation, the Bancroft Library, with its wealth of manuscripts, journals, diaries, local histories, and official orders from viceroys, bishops, governors, priors, and military officials, presents great opportunities for study by students of Spanish-American affairs. Dr. Bolton has even traveled on foot for hundreds of miles to discover facts or verify traditions, as we see in his recent story of Padre Kino, in the interesting book called the *Rim of Christendom*.

Dr. Walter Prescott Webb of the University of Texas presents in *The Great Plains* the interesting theme of the Western plains and the advance of the frontier with the toils, perils, and hardy courage of the pioneers of 1850 and after.

The great treeless plains are more to Dr. Webb than a vast arid or semiarid expanse, for they present an interesting study of physical and historical geography. The ninety-eighth meridian is the entrance to a new world beyond the forest area. This book gives the story of the physical basis of the Great Plains, the native tribes, the coming of the Spaniards, the American approach, the trails, the cattle ranges, the question of water, the six-shooter, the barbed-wire fence, and the literature that has been built up round the cowboy, the cattleman, and the cow-puncher. The book is almost encyclopedic in its wide sweep.

In 1917, on the fiftieth anniversary of its founding, the firm desired a suitable memento. It asked Dr. Ernest C. Moore, at the time professor of education in Harvard University, to present a brief story of the history of education in this country. Dr. Moore accepted the invitation and in the booklet entitled *Fifty Years of Education in America* presented a picture of the wonderful growth and development of the school system of the United States, a development with which the firm had endeavored to keep pace.

CHAPTER TWENTY-FOUR

◇

A PROGRAM FOR READING

THE READING PROGRAM of an educational house is a matter of great moment. Readers (in the elementary list) are the most important single unit from the point of view of the number of copies issued and the financial return.

The first series of the house, the Stickney Readers, was published in 1885. The author was Jenny H. Stickney, principal of the Boston Training School for Teachers, a school that flourished before the Boston Normal School. Miss Stickney soon added a series of supplementary nature books — a series which did not spend its energy in moralizing, but taught the children kindness. Her series led the child to observe and conserve the wild life of birds and animals, a forerunner of a long list of books on this important subject.

In 1892 the house began the publication of the Cyr Readers, written by a gifted teacher, Miss Ellen Cyr of Cambridge, Massachusetts. Miss Cyr's books sought to arouse in the child a love of literature. A certain number of American authors were taken as the basis of each reader. The child visited, as it were, their homes and learned to know them and their works. The Cyr Readers were one of the outstanding successes of the day. So great was their popularity that a Spanish edition was asked for and was immediately published for Spanish-American schools.

Mr. L. H. Jones, president of the Michigan State Normal College, wrote a series of readers that enjoyed two of the greatest successes ever recorded in the publishing world. Through the agency work of Edgar A. DeWitt, the firm's representative in Texas, the Jones Readers were adopted for exclusive use by the State of Texas. The second great adoption of the series was that by the Board of Education for the city of Chicago, secured through the masterly direction of O. J. Laylander, who had charge of the elementary-school work in the great Chicago territory.

Mrs. Ella Flagg Young, Superintendent of Schools of the city of Chicago, and Walter Taylor Field, a specialist in children's reading, were co-authors of a series of readers of unusual literary content and of great appeal to the interests of childhood.

In connection with a series called the Beacon Readers, James H. Fassett, superintendent of the Nashua, New Hampshire, schools, worked out a scientific system of phonetics making use of the initial blend. He taught phonetic principles which enable the reader to pronounce correctly nearly all words of one syllable without the aid of diacritical marks and to divide words into syllables correctly without consulting a dictionary.

The Beacon Readers have been one of Ginn and Company's most successful publications. In a single year half a million copies were sold.

Two prominent teachers of Kansas City, Missouri, Mary E. Pennell and Alice M. Cusack, have written readers which, from the point of view of sales, carry

[188]

the secret of perpetual youth. In view of the careful preparation of the series, involving experiments with fifty thousand children and fifteen hundred teachers, to find the exact status of the child mind in its reaction to reading, we are not surprised that the sale of these carefully graded books, which cover every aspect of elementary work in English reading, has now mounted into millions of copies, and the end is not yet.

Anna Dorothea Cordts is the author of the New Path to Reading. This series is unique in that it presents new words in the first grade through play and dictionary pages with the cartoon type of illustration, emphasizes self-help, and includes material and method for teaching phonics by means of key words.

The Learn to Study Readers, by Dr. Ernest M. Horn of the State University of Iowa, with the assistance of a group of specialists, put emphasis on the work-type of study, with special presentation of factual material and scientifically organized exercises.

For the special use of the Catholic schools the Corona and Rosary Readers present, in carefully graded books, the additional matter for courses that emphasize the religious as well as the secular side of education.

At a meeting of the firm in Columbus a few years ago Dr. Burdette R. Buckingham, at the time director of the Bureau of Educational Research of Ohio State University, was invited to speak on the subject of reading, regarding which he had spent years in making extensive researches. During his presentation of various original points of view, he stated the interesting fact that the existing school readers repeat over and over at least 50 per cent of the same material that had appeared in other readers. Children were therefore given matter to read which they had read before, and schools were paying for material which they already possessed. Dr. Buckingham therefore proposed a novel plan of a series of readers in which 90 per cent of the matter should be entirely new, and the remaining 10 per cent at least new to textbooks. There could then be no duplication of material.

The novel plan was carried out at once. Authors of children's stories and poems, noted juvenile writers of today, were invited to contribute to the series and gladly accepted the offer. The contributions were copyrighted by the company and can never be used in any other series. They cover the whole range of children's interests in stories, poems, and material of scientific, geographical, and biological interest. This plan is carried out in The Children's Bookshelf, which covers the first six years of school life. The volumes of the series are not numbered and have no grade markings. The books have vocabulary control, an interesting style, and a much larger volume of matter than is found in other readers. The result is an unusually rapid progress for the child.

CHAPTER TWENTY-FIVE

◊

THE NEWER TRENDS
IN GEOGRAPHY

To MEET the needs of the modern study of geography and to present the very latest developments in this important school subject, Dr. Wallace W. Atwood in 1917 joined with Alexis Everett Frye in the revision of Frye's Geographies, the success of which series has been described earlier.

Dr. Atwood did his undergraduate work at the University of Chicago, where he also received his degree of Doctor of Philosophy. He specialized in geology and physiography and became associate professor at his Alma Mater. On the retirement of Dr. William M. Davis, professor of geology and physical geography, Dr. Atwood was called to be professor of physiography at Harvard.

Dr. Atwood has taken part in many activities of the United States Geological Survey and other surveys. For many summers, with his fellow geographers and geologists, he led a pack train through the passes of the Rocky Mountains and up the slopes of their towering peaks, tracing the story of the development of the young, rugged mountains and delimiting uncertain boundaries. In 1920 Dr. Atwood became president of Clark University, where he founded a graduate school of geography.

In this connection one is reminded of the medieval institute at Sagres, Portugal, where Prince Henry the Navigator, studying day after day the portolani and globes, sent his vessels to Africa and the south, leading to the discovery of the route around South Africa.

In the *New Geography, Book Two*, of the Frye-Atwood series (published in 1920), Dr. Atwood introduced the concept of regional geography, and the use of regional maps of one simple color-scheme, which has since become a part of modern geography textbooks. With Mrs. Helen Goss Thomas, formerly instructor in geography at Wellesley College and teacher of geography in Harvard University Extension work, Dr. Atwood later launched the Atwood-Thomas series of geographies, the most successful textbooks in this subject in the schools of today.

These geographies, the result of years of testing in the classroom, insist on observation, reasoning, and classroom discussion. They lead to an understanding of how people adapt themselves to the conditions about them. They correlate geography and history. The old-style type of memory lesson has passed away. With the modern series the child cannot fail to see the effect of geographic environment on his life and activities and on those of his fellows. The Atwood-Thomas series emphasizes the human side of geography. With its graphic illustrations and descriptive legends, its scores of regional and other maps, its exercises, projects, tests, workbooks, teachers' manuals, and keys, the Atwood-Thomas series lifts geography to the level of a science, instead of leaving it among the common subjects of the curriculum.

As the Atwood-Thomas Geographies are built on a single-cycle plan which naturally ends with the sixth grade, an interesting problem arose as to the work to be presented for a broad and intelligent economic study of the United States and the world at large in the junior high school, or grades seven and eight.

A common method at the time was the restudy, or review, for the seventh grade of the preceding geography work, an uninteresting, if not repellent, task for both teacher and pupil. In grade eight physical geography and commercial geography filled the year's work with half a year to each subject.

In the Atwood series a new point of view was happily worked out. With the aid of Mr. Thomas F. Power, assistant superintendent of schools, Worcester, Massachusetts, where Dr. Atwood's School of Geography in Clark University is situated, it was decided to try a controlled experiment covering the junior-high-school years.

During the first year of the experiment small committees of progressive teachers from grades seven and eight met and discussed such problems in geography as arise in a fairly large cultural and industrial city with foreign-language problems and, of course, with groups of varying intelligence.

The geography manuscript was carefully studied as to interest, international outlook, economic position of our country, and vocabulary control. It was thereupon actually tested in the classroom in certain schools and in groups divided by intelligence ratings, home environment, and foreign-language backgrounds. Type lessons, pupils' projects, objectives, and outcomes were supplied by alert teachers for the new texts. To these efforts there was a remarkable response by the pupils and their parents.

Probably never before had a series of geographies had as searching an analysis as did the upper books of the Atwood series *The World at Work* and others.

That the result proved the worth of this active co-operation of author, school authority, and progressive teacher is shown by the marvelous success of the books. Incidentally *The World at Work* marked a new milestone in the manufacture of geographies and other textbooks as well. It was the first textbook to be bound in pyroxylin-impregnated (waterproof) book cloth, which has since come into general use.

A series that meets the need of the schools is the Jansen and Allen Geographies. William Jansen was assistant director of the Bureau of Reference and Research in the public-school system of New York City. Miss Nellie B. Allen was formerly a teacher in the Fitchburg Normal School, Massachusetts.

Inasmuch as the New York City educational system has as many pupils as some countries have population, it necessarily requires a carefully prepared course of study, adapted to the conditions that have to be met with children descended from many stocks. It will be recalled that in 1643 Father Jogues found in New Amsterdam eighteen spoken languages, a harbinger of the polyglot conditions of the centuries to come.

Miss Allen had written for the firm the Geographical and Industrial Studies that bear her name, a series of readers with graphic pictures of the countries of the world and the life of their peoples. With the co-operation of Edward K. Robinson, Miss Allen also wrote *Stories and Sketches*, a series which serves as an introduction to geography by giving children in the third and fourth grades a view of young people of other lands and workers in various industries, along with a study of simple forms of both land and water.

Realizing how deeply man is affected by his geographical environment, the aim of the firm has been to meet the needs of the schools not only in the grades but in the high schools and colleges. Many years ago the house published the physical geographies and *Meteorology* by Professor William M. Davis of Harvard, an outstanding authority on these subjects. *The Earth and Its History*, by Dr. John Hodgdon Bradley, Jr., of the University of Montana, opens wide the door to a most interesting study of geology and anthropology. As the reader peruses this work "scenery will take on a new meaning; time will no longer be viewed in the light of man-written history; the earth will become more than a mere abode." Professor Charles C. Colby of the University of Chicago and Miss Alice Foster of the same university are the authors of *Economic Geography*, for secondary schools. In this book they illustrate how nations make use of the land and the resources about them.

[197]

Professor Preston E. James of the University of Michigan wrote *Outlines of Geography*, which describes and emphasizes cultural background. Professor Roderick Peattie of Ohio State University produced his *New College Geography*, carrying this most interesting subject to a higher intellectual plateau; Professor Hervey Woodburn Shimer of the Massachusetts Institute of Technology, in *An Introduction to Earth History*, gave a graphic view of paleontology as shown in the development of the constantly changing earth and in the life of plants and animals.

Charles B. Fawcett, in *A Political Geography of the British Empire*, presents a scientific study of what has been called the greatest experiment in human organization that the world has yet seen. In their *Commercial and Industrial Geography*, Albert G. Keller, professor of the science of society, and Avard Longley Bishop, professor of business administration, both of Yale University, show how production and trade are the natural outgrowth of man's need for food, clothing, and shelter.

These are a few of the textbooks which the firm has presented in the field of geography and allied subjects.

For many years it has been the practice to have the state supplements to geography bound in a general edition of the upper book of a geography series, a costly proceeding, requiring, as it does, the carrying of twenty or more editions of a book to meet the needs of the leading states.

[198]

In 1918 the firm's Wisconsin agent was Lynn B. Stiles, a trained educator and psychologist. To meet the needs for a more exhaustive study of the geography of Wisconsin, Mr. Stiles evolved a workbook to accompany the regular general edition. This workbook took the place of the State supplement and furnished much fuller and more interesting material for the pupil. This ingenious device provided tests, map-drawing, local history, and a complete map of the State in color.

Aside from books in series, there are some single volumes that have notably contributed to American culture and intelligence. Gayley's *Classic Myths in English Literature*, first published in 1893, like the stories it tells, can never grow old. It was written by Professor Charles Mills Gayley of the University of California. In this volume of charming format we find the myths of the Greeks, Romans, Norsemen, and Germans, the gods of Olympus, of the Elysian Fields, and of Valhalla, as they are found in English literature.

Another book that has held its place down the years is *Folkways*, by the late William Graham Sumner of Yale. The book is a scholarly, thorough, and scientific study of the mores of primitive peoples. Dr. Albert G. Keller, a pupil of Sumner's, became so deeply interested in *Folkways* that he wrote for the house a volume entitled *Colonization*, a searching study of the founding of new societies.

A book of great importance on the subject of philosophy was Dr. William Turner's *History of Philosophy*. Dr. Turner was professor of philosophy in St. Paul Seminary and, later, professor of the same subject in the Catholic University of America. Dr. Turner's book treats of schools and systems of philosophy, Oriental, Greek, Roman, patristic, scholastic, and modern. The book emphasizes in particular the history of scholasticism (arising under the Carolingians), which had so great an influence on the thirteenth and fourteenth centuries — the era of Alcuin, John Scotus Erigena, Gerbert, Anselm, Abélard, Aquinas, Roger Bacon, and Alexander of Hales. Turner gives a graphic explanation of the later philosophers and humanists, — Descartes, Kant, Hegel, to those of the present day, — a presentation of the subject which concerns the ultimate principle and laws of all things.

Everybody needs money; but precious few know anything about it, save the vital matter of immediate receipts and expenditures. In 1895, a year before the days of Bryan's "cross of gold" and "sixteen to one," Horace White published a book called *Money and Banking*, to open the eyes of the student and general reader to the history of currency from the earliest days to the present. No fewer than five times has White's book been revised, to keep pace with the panics of 1893, 1907, and 1929, the new currency acts of Congress, the Federal Reserve System, the guaranty of bank deposits, the passing of the gold standard, international

[200]

exchange, war debts, and hundreds of other problems that new legislation presents to the citizen year by year. Since the death of Mr. White the book has been again revised by Dean Charles S. Tippetts of the University of Pittsburgh and Professor Lewis A. Froman of the University of Buffalo.

In a recent number of a leading preparatory-school magazine there appeared a silhouette representing a night scene of a dormitory with every window brilliantly lighted. Through an open window could be seen a student poring intently over the books on his table, his hands on his head, with a bright light shining on his work. It would be a fairly good guess that one of his books was the latest volume of the College Entrance Examinations.

Up to 1899 it was the general custom for colleges to give their own examinations to pupils seeking entrance to the freshman class. (The entrance to state universities was, as a rule, through certification from the high schools.)

In 1900, after considerable study, about thirty colleges and universities of the country formed a board which yearly thereafter prepared a uniform examination on all subjects required for entrance to college.

A student who was successful in these examinations received a certificate which was, in fact, a passport for entrance to any college or university.

For thirty-seven years Ginn and Company has been the official publisher of the board.

◆

CHAPTER TWENTY-SIX

THE PROGRESS OF SCIENCE

BEFORE the year 1886 the work in science in the high school left much to be desired. In physics, pupils had to be content with text-books that were scarcely more than pleasing story-books; indeed, a high-school physics of the late seventies explained the law of gravitation as follows:

"Herschel tells an amusing story of a man who attempted to walk on water by means of large cork boots. Scarcely, however, had he ventured out, ere the law of gravitation seized him, and all that could be seen was a pair of human heels, whose movements manifested a great state of uneasiness in the human appendage below."

At that time it was a rarity for a pupil to handle a piece of physical apparatus. He saw from afar something happening under a vacuum pump manipulated by the teacher. Laboratories in the true sense of the word were well-nigh nonexistent. The world had not yet realized the social significance of science. Alfred P. Gage was at this time instructor in physics in the English High School of Boston. He wrote for the house *Elements of Physics*, based on the method of teaching through experiment. His motto was "Read nature in the language of experiment." Beyond the general laws of physics, the pupil was led to seek out for himself the problems of the day's lesson by personal investigation, with the use of simple apparatus. The doctrine of the conservation of energy

[205]

was prominent throughout the text. Principles and laws were preceded by questions leading up to these principles and laws. The pupil was asked to observe and to think.

It is a somewhat far cry from Gage to Millikan and Gale. In no activity of man has more rapid progress been made than in the domains of physics and chemistry. Consider for a moment what the single department of sound is doing for the human race in the radio alone. To keep abreast with the constant advance in the teaching of physics, the firm aimed high and secured in 1906 the services of Millikan and Gale, both of the University of Chicago. Their *First Course in Physics* was received with immediate favor and has for all these intervening years been a recognized standard textbook on the subject. Both of the authors have become men of distinction. Dr. Robert A. Millikan in 1923 received the Nobel prize and has otherwise been widely honored. For many years he has been president of the California Institute of Technology. Dr. Henry G. Gale is today chairman of the department of physics and dean of the division of the physical sciences at the University of Chicago. On the latest revision of the physics they had the collaboration of James P. Coyle, head of the Department of Physics, Lane Technical High School, Chicago. With the collaboration of Charles William Edwards they published a widely used textbook in physics for colleges. Two other books of distinction with Millikan's name on the title page are Millikan and Mills's *Electricity, Sound, and Light* and Millikan, Roller, and Watson's *Mechanics, Molecular Physics, Heat, and Sound*.

The application of physics to the problems of daily life is today the aim of physicists. On the pages of these books the pupil sees the faces of the great world physicists, investigators, and inventors, among them Galileo, Faraday, Beebe, Einstein, Michelson, Edison, the Wright brothers, Marconi, and others — men whose studies and experiments have solved mysteries beyond even the dreams of earlier investigators for the mastery of the physical world.

Books on the various phases of physics and allied subjects for high schools, colleges, and technical schools, laboratory manuals, thermodynamics, theoretical mechanics, written by leading scholars of the day, were published by the Athenaeum Press. If the past three hundred years (says Dr. Millikan) is an index of the next three hundred, the supreme question of mankind may then be of how the application of the scientific method can be best stimulated and accelerated in all departments of human life.

Many decades ago the American people were awakened to the need of pure foods, inspired in part by the work of Lewis B. Allyn ("the little white-haired man" of the Westfield (Massachusetts) State Normal School), whose book *Elementary Applied Chemistry* was published by the house. At that time little attention was paid to the adulteration of foods, which

[207]

was widespread, as was proved later, to an alarming degree. In his classwork Mr. Allyn insisted on the value of a laboratory test of food products. The pupils were asked to buy, in different stores, ice cream and other things that were supposed to contain flavoring extracts of pure quality.

The test revealed astonishing results. From the coal-tar and other dyes extracted, large pieces of cloth were colored in the brilliant hues of the spectrum and were hung up to the view of the citizens. The result was a storm, which Mr. Allyn calmly rode by telling the merchants to use only pure foods and saying he would co-operate with them. This work in Westfield may be said to have been the forerunner of new laws looking to the awakening of the American people to the question of pure foods and the preservation of the general health. In effect, it removed untold dangers from the lives, not of guinea pigs, but of a hundred million neighbors and fellow citizens.

In 1887 the firm published Joseph Y. Bergen's *Elements of Botany*. Bergen was an instructor in botany in the English High School of Boston.

As in the other sciences of this school, Bergen emphasized experimental work that could be easily carried on in the classroom. Being a practical teacher, he used in the laboratory such materials as could be easily obtained. For his textbook he secured interesting illustrations, superior as teaching-materials to those of any other textbook of the day.

[208]

HENRY GORDON GALE

ROBERT ANDREWS MILLIKAN

OTIS W. CALDWELL

The matter of plant diseases and the effect of these diseases on the food supply became in later years a matter of serious moment. William Boyce Thompson, recognizing the danger, founded and endowed in Yonkers, for the study of plant diseases, the institute that bears his name. This holds the same relation to the plant world that the Rockefeller Foundation does to human life.

Bergen, Dr. Otis W. Caldwell, and Dr. Bradley M. Davis of the University of Michigan foresaw many years ago the trend that was likely to take place in the study of botany, and provided for it in their textbooks by introducing and presenting the study of plant-breeding, plant diseases, bacteria, forestry, and gardening.

The name of Otis W. Caldwell is one to conjure by in the teaching of science. Dr. Caldwell graduated at Franklin College and received his degree of Doctor of Philosophy from the University of Chicago. He held for a time the chair of biology in the Eastern Illinois State Normal School and then became professor of botany and dean of the University High School in the University of Chicago.

It was in the field of general science, however, that he was to win his laurels. In answer to a question on science his interesting response was as follows:

" Each human generation seems to have its wonders, which surpass the things of common experience. We build higher buildings, deeper and longer tunnels, fly higher, farther, or for a longer time. We cause chemistry, biology, or physics to do things which were recently called impossible. We see so far into space that we make our own earth almost nothing in the space it occupies, yet it is still the home for the minds which discover such wonderful things. Man is a fearless and adventurous animal, always seeking to try something which no person before has succeeded in doing, and always wanting to know what nobody has yet learned. He is restless in the presence of things achieved, always eager to carry his flashlight of experimentation and investigation into unexplored places, so that light and knowledge may dispel darkness and ignorance. He is always endeavoring to push back the borders of the unknown. His inquiring and daring mind is in itself a scientific fact of the greatest significance."

To test his ideas, Dr. Caldwell had a remarkable opportunity as he developed the Lincoln School of Teachers College, Columbia University. Admission to the school was selective. It was a cross section of the community, and required of every child a dual activity — work with the brain and work with the hands. After some hours the pupil went from the desk to the laboratory or the workshop. Every movement in the school was related to fact. The turning of a doorknob was an illustration of the resultant of forces.

The outstanding position of Dr. Caldwell in the field of education is that of champion of general science. There had been for years an increasing interest in the teaching of science in high-school courses, since it was evident that science entered into all fields of human experience. The work, however, was carried on largely through specialized, unrelated, and abstract courses, and with unsatisfactory results. Dr. Caldwell believed and taught that science in the junior high schools should be based not on specialized science courses, but on those broad units of science that touch the everyday life of the pupil and the citizen.

By using this everyday-life appeal, the pupil might be led to careful and accurate observation. He might recognize in one or another of the sciences presented to him a field for his particular interest. The teaching of the science must be accurate so far as it went, and must be interesting if it was to appeal to the everyday life and observations of the child. There must be nothing to unlearn, if the child was to advance farther into the realm of science.

The results of careful study and of many years of experimentation by Dr. Caldwell appeared in his *Elements of General Science*, written in collaboration with William L. Eikenberry, at that time connected with the University of Kansas. This book was adopted at once in hundreds of schools, and won for general science a place in the curriculum of the junior high school, a place so definite and secure that it is now taken for granted. The simplicity of the units causes us to wonder that general science was so long on the way. These units include air, water and its uses, work,

[211]

energy, electricity, the earth in relation to other astronomical bodies, the earth's crust, and life upon the earth. Simple as the units appear, they cover nearly the entire range of ordinary human experience.

Dr. Caldwell's associate in his later books was Dr. Francis D. Curtis of the University of Michigan, who had made the study of general science a part of his lifework. The new *Science for Today*, by Caldwell and Curtis, is a distinct tribute to progress.

Probably nothing can better illustrate the progress of science in the schools than a comparison of *General Science*, of twenty-three years ago, with *Science for Today*. The repeated presence of the term "energy" in the new book is noteworthy. Radio, the by-products of petroleum, refrigeration, the periscope, the airplane, and radium are words that indicate the onward march of science.

The kindred subject of chemistry has been represented in the Ginn list as fully as physics. The earliest work published by the house on this subject was Williams's chemistry. Williams was a fellow teacher with Gage in the English High School, Boston. The ever-increasing application of chemistry to the daily needs of the people in food, arts, and industry required an intensive study of the subject and an authoritative authorship in any text that hoped to meet the rapidly growing needs of the day.

Chemistry moved onward, with exacting methods of inquiry, in the study of the transmutation of elements

[212]

WILLIAM EDWARDS HENDERSON   THOMAS E. MASON

WILLIAM MCPHERSON

(*pace* the ancient alchemist), radioactivity, protons, deuterons, neutrons, alpha particles, parahydrogen, and mass spectrum-analysis. Two professors, William McPherson and William Edward Henderson, of Ohio State University, leaders in the field of the new chemistry, prepared *An Elementary Study of Chemistry*, which met the needs of the many students who came to college with no knowledge of the subject. This text was followed by a college text, *A Course in General Chemistry*, which was so widely accepted by the colleges that its use has been for years well-nigh universal. It has been one of the greatest successes of the house. Few advances in the unlimited field of chemistry have escaped the researches of these scientists. In the preparation of their high-school text, *Chemistry for Today*, they were associated with George W. Fowler, supervisor of science in the city schools of Syracuse, New York. A still newer book by these three authors — *Chemistry at Work* — presents the very latest advances in this subject.

A widely known name in astronomy was that of Professor Charles A. Young, whose father had been famous as an astronomer at Dartmouth (where his illustrious son also taught the science) and had been the leading authority of his time on the study of the sun. In 1888 he published his *General Astronomy*, for colleges, and two years later his *Lessons in Astronomy*. His high-school texts were, in general, free from mathematics, but they nevertheless gave a clear view of the subject. Even the legends and mythology were added for the use

[213]

of pupils who otherwise would probably never meet these interesting stories in their high-school courses.

Professor Charles A. Young retired from Dartmouth to accept the chair of astronomy at Princeton. Here he was succeeded by Professors Russell, Dugan, and Stewart, who, following the Young tradition, wrote the textbook *Astronomy*.

When we lift our eyes to the gorgeous panorama of the starry heavens, with the planets moving in their distant orbits and the moon affecting the tides, and when by day we watch the sun constantly changing our climate, our rainfall, and our dust bowls, we might well question whether the frontiers of human knowledge are not being retarded if we relegate astronomy to an inconsequential place in inconsequential electives.

In many high-school courses biology is a *sine qua non* in the curriculum. In seeking for a satisfactory text in biology the firm turned to Dr. Curtis, to Dr. Caldwell, and to Nina H. Sherman of the University High School of Ann Arbor, Michigan. Dr. Curtis is head of the department of science, University High School, and professor of the teaching of science, University of Michigan. The fruit of the labors of these authors is *Biology for Today*, a book which is authoritative and which shows extensive research in the laboratory as well as years of experimentation in the classroom, being based on the thoroughly modern fundamental idea of energy as related to biology and its effect on living things.

[214]

Dr. Benjamin C. Gruenberg, director of the American Association for Medical Progress, had presented to the firm, while he was still a teacher of science in a high school of New York City, a manuscript that was immediately recognized as having unusual merit. It was the first successful effort to present to the high-school student a functional view of biology. The book was published under the title *Elementary Biology*, and has since been followed by Dr. Gruenberg's *Biology and Human Life*, which applies biology to daily life.

These textbooks, with the modern Meier and Shoemaker's *Essentials of Biology*, show the essential unity of life processes among animals and plants. They also show the correlation of physiology and morphology, the application of morphology to daily life, the principles of genetics and eugenics, and the methods of improving the life of plants and animals — all with new photographs and diagrams.

Two important works in physics carry the name of Oscar M. Stewart, professor of physics in the University of Missouri. Stewart's *Physics* was written as a popular first course for colleges. In its pages the student finds mechanics, magnetism, electricity, light, heat, properties of matter, and sound — topics which, with many others, lead to advanced work. With Burton L. Cushing and Judson R. Towne as co-authors, *Physics for Secondary Schools* covers the work in a progressive way for the high-school student.

[215]

CHAPTER TWENTY-SEVEN

◇

NATURE STUDY

THE WORLD OF MUSIC

IN ITS early days the house had published, as we have seen, *Nature Stories*, by Miss Stickney. These were simple tales that led the child into God's great out-of-doors. Miss Stickney was a pioneer in presenting nature study to children.

In 1900 was begun William J. Long's Wood Folk Series, which carried on the general idea. Dr. Long is a lover of nature, of wild life, and of the big woods, and has a keen power of observation. His style in writing is simple and interesting, and his stories hold the attention of the child.

" Hast thou named all the birds without a gun?
Loved the wood-rose and left it on its stalk? "

asks Emerson. Dr. Long could answer Yes. There are in his books no description of beautiful batteries, no tales of the bullet going with deadly precision to the heart of an inoffensive wild beast. In his presence in the woods the quail rests peacefully on her nest; the loon rejoices in the still lake; the deer crops the grass, the leaves, and the lily pads without fear.

As for Dr. Long's philosophy, we may give it in his own words:

" To the hunter without a gun, there is no closed season on any game; and a doe and her fawns are far better hunting than a ten-point buck. By land or water he is always ready; there are no labors for effects, except what he chooses to impose upon himself; no disappointments are possible, for whether his game be still, or on the jump; shy as a wilderness raven, or as full of curiosity as a blue jay; he always finds something to stow away in his heart, where he keeps things he loves to remember. . . . The very best thing that can be said for the hunter without a gun is this: ' The wilderness and the solitary place shall be glad for him,' for something of the gentle spirit of Saint Francis comes with him, and when he goes he leaves no pain, nor death, nor fear of man behind him."

Year by year a charming nature story was looked for by teacher, pupil, and general reader. For them appeared *A Little Brother to the Bear*, *Secrets of the Woods*, *Ways of Wood Folk*, *Wilderness Ways*, and *Wood Folk at School*, showing the everyday life of the birds and animals of the forest. The books were illustrated with the inimitable pictures of Charles Copeland, himself a lover of nature, with as deep a sympathy for wild life as Dr. Long himself.

As much as any other author of his day, Dr. Long aided in developing in the school child a love of nature and of nature's creatures, and the house of Ginn was happy indeed in doing its share in promoting the movement for bird sanctuaries, game preserves, and the development of societies, like the Audubon, to preserve our feathered songsters and the wild life of the forest.

In 1936 the house began publishing The World of Music, probably the most ambitious series ever presented to the educational world. It consists of eight

A COPELAND ILLUSTRATION

distinct and complete courses of music instruction, as follows: kindergarten course; elementary vocal course; junior high school vocal course; course for consolidated and rural schools; piano course; band course; orchestra course; and music appreciation course.

The editors of these courses are Mabelle Glenn, director of public-school music, Kansas City, Missouri; Helen S. Leavitt, instructor in music, Boston University and The Wheelock School, Boston; Victor L. F. Rebmann, director of the department of music, Ithaca College, Ithaca, New York; Earl L. Baker, formerly director of public-school music department, Lawrence College, Appleton, Wisconsin; Marguerite V. Hood, University of Montana, Missoula; Glenn Gildersleeve, state director of music education, Delaware; Charles B. Righter, associate professor of music, State University of Iowa, Iowa City; William D. Revelli, director of bands and assistant professor of wind instruments, University of Michigan, Ann Arbor; William C. Hartshorn, director of junior and senior high school music, Los Angeles; Bess Daniels, department of music, Ithaca College, Ithaca; and art editor, C. Valentine Kirby, state director of art education, Pennsylvania. Elbridge W. Newton, pronounced by a leading university music authority as one of the nation's most profound scholars in music, served as managing editor. In preparing the course Miss Helen Leavitt aided Mr. Newton in a marked degree through her wide knowledge of music and her experience in the classroom and in the lecture hall.

Many music educators and musicians contributed advice and assistance in the development of The World of Music. The list of the eight courses which it includes indicates that this series covers all music activities in the schools from kindergarten through junior high school.

The many folk songs were gathered by folk-song experts all over the world. The composed songs represent not only the master writers but also noted contemporary American composers. Pictorial art is correlated with music and poetry by the presentation of famous pictures.

Through this series the study of music is integrated with other school subjects in order that music may enrich the entire curriculum and be enriched by it.

A forward step in typography was taken by the house as early as 1923. In that year four titles had been issued in the Music Education Series, which continued the line of succession of the Mason system. In the pages of these books and also in others issued later in the series, there was an important typographic improvement. The plates of the books were made by the cerographic, or wax, process, a relief process used at that time in making the plates of colored maps and also the diagrams for scientific books. This method of making music plates had been suggested to an engraver a few years before by our technical department. It was first used in some issues of the Coda, a series of supplementary music pamphlets published by the company. After two experimental issues in 1917 the process was found to be very successful.

The great advantage of this method over the typographic method, which had been employed for many years, lay in the fact that desirable features of lithographed music could be reproduced in an electrotype plate for relief-printing. The staff lines, the phrase marks, the extended cross-strokes, the ties, and the slurs — instead of being composed of small pieces as in typographic composition, a process which inevitably resulted in their showing breaks and wear after slight use — were now all continuous, unbroken lines, as when lithographed. Then, too, a much greater freedom was possible in the choice of shapes for the characters than when the typographic method was used.

The plates of our latest music books, the World of Music series, are made by still another method, one which combines (also with excellent results) the advantages of the typographic and lithographic methods of reproduction in plates for relief-printing.

The growth of the science of education, with the ever-widening development of normal schools and teachers' colleges, requires the progressive textbook publisher to maintain a constant surveillance to meet the demands of the schools. Besides the works for teachers, which we have already mentioned, in mathematics, history, and science, the development of the junior high school and its aims led to the publication of *Junior High School Procedure*, by Frank C. Touton of the University of Southern California and Alice Ball Struthers of the Thomas Starr King Junior High School, Los Angeles.

Carpenter and Rufi wrote *The Teacher and Secondary-School Administration*; Clapp, Chase, and Merriman, *Introduction to Education*; Dolch, *The Psychology and Teaching of Reading*; Eikenberry and Waldron, *Educational Biology*; Engelhardt, *Public School Organization and Administration*; Judd, *Psychology of Secondary Education*; Koos, *The American Secondary School*; Norton and Norton, *Foundations for Curriculum Building*; Rugg, *American Life and the School Curriculum*; Saucier, *Introduction to Modern Views of Education*; Knight, *Education in the United States*; and Umstattd, *Secondary-School Teaching*. These are a few of the texts that are designed to show the results of recent study and the activities of progressive minds in the field of public education.

◇

EXTENSION OF MEMBERSHIP
IN THE FIRM

FOR MANY years Fred B. Ginn covered the territory of the central West with special reference to colleges. This work was greatly to his fancy. Like his brother Edwin, he was devoted to the classics, and in the high schools and colleges of the West he planted far and wide the Latin and Greek books of the firm. Fred Ginn was a commanding figure. In his young manhood he had been a captain in the Civil War, and at its close, as we have seen, he joined his brother in the foundation of a new publishing house. Tall, with white beard, straight as an Indian chief, urbane and kindly to an unwonted degree, he was an impressive figure wherever he went. He was welcomed by college president and by fledgling instructor. Desiring to reside on the Pacific coast, he was given charge of that territory. For years he went up and down that storied land enriched by the memories of Drake, Portolá, Junípero Serra, Captain Gray, John McLaughlin, Sutter, Sloat, Montgomery, and Stockton.

The vast distances and the rapid growth of schools and colleges led him to ask for an assistant, and Selden C. Smith was sent to the coast from the New England field. Selden Smith was a native of Vermont. He graduated at Dartmouth in 1897, and after a brief sojourn in New England went in response to the call from California. He did agency work there until the death of Fred B. Ginn, when he took charge of the San Francisco office. In 1909 he became a member of the firm. With Smith's indefatigable labor and a personality that everywhere won friends for the house, the Pacific coast thrived mightily, Washington, Oregon, Utah, Idaho, Montana, Arizona, and the Hawaiian Islands having been added to the San Francisco field since Smith took charge.

The high-school and college work in the New York field had been so widely developed by Mr. Conant that he also needed assistance. Frederick C. Hodgdon was called to New York from the New England field. Mr. Hodgdon was a graduate of Tufts College, of which he is a trustee. As an undergraduate he had charge of the book room, and to keep sufficient stock he had to go often to Boston. As in the story said to have been told by Emerson of the path to the mousetrap-maker's cabin in the woods, Hodgdon's practical path had led to the house of Ginn, where he secured for his stockroom the books so eagerly awaited (let us hope) by impatient students. On receiving his degree Mr. Hodgdon took the well-known path, and offered his services to the house. With the keen discernment that formed so marked a characteristic of his being, Austin Kenerson saw in Hodgdon the manifest possibilities of an outstanding agent, and Hodgdon was appointed to the New England field, only to be called in a short time to New York.

His work in the high-school and college field was unusual. A ripe scholar, he studied high-school subjects with deep care, and he knew from every angle

[228]

the books he offered to teachers. Few men knew better than he the intricate problems of the New York Regents' system. He brought to the schools a knowledge of what was called for by educational authorities and what was in general the trend of the times. He was welcomed in every department of education in the states he visited, and his reports of conditions to the house were models of clarity. He was admitted to the firm in 1912, and remained until his retirement in 1931. For years the impetus of his work has been a continuing source of noble influence for the house.

In 1906, when Gilson was transferred to the Boston office, O. J. Laylander went to Chicago to assume direction of the agency work in the elementary field. No happier choice could have been made. Laylander was born in a log house in rural Ohio, where the opportunities for school education were very limited, but where the education of the eye, ear, mind, and hand from observation and labor was unlimited. In a pioneer normal school he caught some glimpses of the philosophy of teaching. Laylander's father had named him Orange Judd out of admiration for the well-known editor of the *American Agriculturist*. On arriving at adolescence Laylander shortened his name to O. J., by which he has been known from that day to this. So widely was this unusual combination known that a letter addressed merely O. J., Chicago, Illinois, promptly reached him, a tribute as well to the marvelous efficiency of our postal service.

Laylander's father was deeply devoted to farming, as shown by the name given to his son. He believed in the future of the great West, the West beyond the Mississippi, and he secured a section of land in Iowa for his boy. Thereupon Laylander went West, perhaps, he thought, to fame and fortune.

The plow had never touched the Iowa acres since Adam was a small boy. A Sanskrit sacred book says, " The hand of God is in the five," but the German adage says, " Of all good things there are three." Laylander was to prove the falsity of the latter adage. He remained three years on the farm, but nothing was good. Drought one year, blizzards the next, and insect pests beyond the computation of the Arabic notation the third discouraged the youth.

The Eclogues of Virgil are beautiful — in the classroom. Laylander abandoned the farm and became a teacher. In time the mantle of superintendent was placed on his shoulders. For twelve years he was superintendent in Cedar Falls, Iowa. As teacher and superintendent, he came to know the Ginn elementary list. He was particularly impressed by the novelty and principles enunciated by Frye in his geographies, since they agreed exactly with his ideas on this important subject. He spoke frequently before teachers' institutes. In 1900 he entered the Iowa agency field for the house, and six years later became manager in Chicago of the Western territory for elementary-school work. In 1909 he became a member of the firm.

Since 1931, when he became an inactive partner, he has spent a large part of his time, except in winter, at his home on Burt Lake, northern Michigan. Here, in the love of nature, he holds communion, as Bryant says, with her visible forms. In the companionship of good books and friends he finds the hours pass all too quickly. James Jeffrey Roche appreciated the philosophy of life when he wrote

> " Crept the minutes for the sad,
>   Sped the cycles for the glad,
> But the march of time was neither less nor more."

Time does not seem to march for Laylander.

In 1883 Mr. Plimpton received a letter from a teacher in Texas asking for a position in the agency force of Ginn and Company. The writer was Edgar A. DeWitt. DeWitt was born in Massachusetts and graduated at Dartmouth. Going to Texas to teach, he became interested in the pressing educational problems of the South. He was later engaged by the house. An office was opened in Dallas, and DeWitt carried on the work of the firm for more than four decades, with a success and an ability that were outstanding in agency annals. He became a partner in 1914, and sixteen years later retired. There had been built up during the years an ever-increasing business in high schools and colleges in the South; but DeWitt made the house an active factor in every branch of the business, elementary as well as high-school and college.

[231]

Up to this time few Southern educators had presented manuscripts for publication. Most of the firm's authors were from the North. DeWitt wished to see his house a national one, and he took the broad view that in no subject might a more promising beginning be made toward a national point of view than in the subject of American history. It is safe to say that at that time no history written by a Northern author could have any sale in the South. It was still too near Appomattox and the era of reconstruction.

DeWitt presented a manuscript on American history written by three Texas authors: Oscar H. Cooper, superintendent of schools at Galveston; Harry F. Estill of the Sam Houston State Normal Institute; and Leonard Lemmon, superintendent of schools at Sherman. The manuscript showed that it was possible for historical scholars and teachers to view national events in a broad, philosophical way, without partisan bias or distortion of facts. The book was a success; and Ginn and Company became, so to speak, a national institution; for on its list have appeared in the last thirty years the names of many of the leaders in school and college throughout the South. Once a year, at Christmas, it was DeWitt's custom to write a letter of good cheer and well wishes to his myriad of friends in the schools of the South. His literary ability made each letter a welcome greeting. To DeWitt may be paid the honor of securing the exclusive adoption of the Jones Readers for the entire State of Texas, no doubt the largest possible exclusive adoption in a single subject in America.

For many years the directing force in six of the Southern states was Linton Burnett Robeson, who was born in North Carolina and graduated at Emory College. He taught school at various places in Georgia, and became an agent of the house under the direction of E. C. Branson, who had at the time general direction of Ginn and Company's affairs in the Southeastern states. Branson was an able educator, as well as a successful textbook representative, and he found in Robeson an able coadjutor. After a few years Branson resigned to resume the work of education, and Robeson succeeded him in the direction of affairs.

Robeson has a vigorous personality. He studied all the angles of his work, since from the very beginning there was active competition in his field. He knew his books thoroughly, and had an oratorical power which impressed the State and other committees before which he was called to explain his texts. His hospitality has ever been of the generous Southern type, which knows no limit. His winter home in Florida, on the Homosassa River, partakes of the nature of a medieval barony, without the discomforts that proverbially are characteristic of baronies. In 1914 he became a partner, and remained the directing force in the vast area of six Southern states until he retired to the inactive list.

[233]

Closely associated with Robeson for many years was Norman C. Miller, who was born in Georgia, and also graduated at Emory College, Robeson's Alma Mater.

After graduation Miller entered the educational field, in which he worked for seven years. Accidentally meeting one of the Ginn partners from the North who was at that time on a visit to the South, Miller was induced to give up teaching and to enter active agency work under Robeson. The plan was an ideal one, as a remarkable friendship had existed between Robeson and his young lieutenant since college days.

In 1920 Miller became a partner, and on Robeson's retirement was in sole charge of the Atlanta office and field. Mr. Miller died in 1935.

The Athenaeum Press was built in 1896 (as we have seen) by Lewis Parkhurst, and was directed by him for more than ten years. In 1906 Mark R. Jouett was called to take up a part of the burden. Jouett graduated from Harvard in 1903. For the next few years he was an agent in the high-school field of Connecticut and New York, where his broad human sympathy, quiet culture, and keen mind endeared him to the school authorities and teachers, to whom he was always a welcome visitor.

In this world some men have the *wanderlust*; others, in traveling, experience *heimweh*. Jouett did not like to travel. The work of supervising a great press was the type of activity he ardently longed for, and Parkhurst was greatly pleased to invite him to share the daily, if not hourly, responsibilities that the Athenaeum Press, with its many departments, entails.

With thousands upon thousands of books issuing daily from its modern presses, with its intricate binding machines, its composition work in many languages, its delicate electric mechanism, its problems of the health and well-being of the employees, Jouett at once found opportunity for every play of his activities, mental and physical. As one looks at the Press from across the historic Charles, one sees the great structure built by Parkhurst and later carried on by Jouett. *Si monumentum requiris, circumspice.* In 1917 Jouett became a member of the firm. In the same year John W. Swartz was admitted to the firm, after eleven years of active agency work for the Columbus office, a field which covered the great States of Ohio, Kentucky, and West Virginia. Swartz resigned in 1930.

The rapid growth of business in the elementary schools in the New York field brought into the agency force LeRoy J. Weed, whose birthplace was far above Cayuga's waters, in Ithaca, named, perhaps, from the classic isle, the home of "the much-enduring divine Ulysses." Weed graduated from the venerable Union College, of which he later became a trustee. (The use of *venerable* is permissible when one recalls that Union is one hundred and forty-three years old and was at one time the second largest college in the United States.)

After leaving college Weed became a teacher in one of the leading preparatory schools of the East,

[235]

a training which is generally acknowledged to be of more positive value than the work done in college. If a man wishes to find out how little he knows of a subject, he should start teaching it.

Weed's agency work has been largely in New York, New Jersey, and Pennsylvania, at first under the direction of Richard S. Thomas. He was admitted to the firm in 1918. Weed's territory embraces millions. It is a microcosm so far as New York City is concerned, a union of stocks from all quarters of the globe, eager to receive the benefit of a free education, ranging from the primary grade to the senior class of college, all under the able and efficient direction of a Board of Superintendents.

Weed understands thoroughly the needs of the schools. He can speak both the language of educators and the language of statesmen; for he served the State of New York in the legislature at Albany, where from inside the breastworks he learned something of how the wheels of government go round.

Henry P. Conway, affectionately known to his myriad of friends as Pat, graduated at Dartmouth in the class of 1897. He was born in Oldtown, Maine. After graduation he first became a teacher in Vermont and then, going West, taught in Minnesota and Wisconsin. In the meantime, by assiduous labor, he had passed his bar examinations in Minnesota. There arose in the West in 1903 the need of additional agents for the rapidly growing business, and Conway was

(STANDING) F. C. HODGDON, H. P. CONWAY, L. J. WEED, M. H. JENCKS, A. L. PRIDDY, M. R. JOUETT, J. W. SWARTZ, E. H. KENERSON, D. W. HALL, S. C. SMITH

(SEATED) E. A. DEWITT, T. B. LAWLER, O. J. LAYLANDER, H. H. HILTON, G. A. PLIMPTON, C. H. THURBER, L. PARKHURST, N. C. MILLER, R. S. THOMAS, L. B. ROBESON

invited to join the agency ranks of the firm. He accepted, and brought to his new duties a mind steeped in the classics and also a wide grasp of mathematics.

Far and wide he traveled through the great states of the West, from the Dakotas to the Rio Grande and from the Appalachians to the Golden Gate. He was a student of educational problems, speaking frequently at teachers' institutes, especially on English and the modern aspect of the teaching of geography. He became a partner in 1920, and on the retirement of Mr. Laylander was given charge of the elementary work in the Chicago field. In his death, in 1932, the firm lost one of its most successful members.

When the much-loved Austin H. Kenerson died in 1905, his son, Edward H. Kenerson, had been for two years on the agency staff. Kenerson graduated at Dartmouth, and at once became an agent. His field was New Hampshire and Vermont. He later became the manager of the Boston field, which covers all New England except Connecticut. In 1920 he was admitted to the firm. Kenerson's work has covered a wide range — elementary school, high school, and college, all of which has given him a broad grasp of the whole textbook situation. The closely knit New England territory has brought him in direct contact with superintendents, supervisors, and other school administrators. Like his father, he has built up a close relationship with them. On the death of Mr. Priddy he became treasurer of the firm.

CHAPTER TWENTY-NINE

◇

HEALTH,
CIVICS,
AND AGRICULTURE

THE EVER-INCREASING attention given to the matter of health by individual, city, state, or nation demands an ever-growing amount of time and study on the part of the schools, to promote healthful living and the formation of healthful habits. The early publications of Blaisdell were followed by the Gulick Hygiene Series. The Andress Health Series began to appear in 1924, edited by Dr. J. Mace Andress, formerly of the State Normal College of Salem, Massachusetts. With him were associated six health specialists and leaders of health education: Dr. W. A. Evans, formerly of Northwestern University, Mabel C. Bragg of Boston University, Annie Turner Andress, Julia E. Dickson of Teachers College of the City of Boston, Maud A. Brown of the University of Kansas, and Dr. I. H. Goldberger of the New York City public schools.

The titles tell the story of the new day in health education: *Summer Fun, The Sunshine School, A Journey to Health Land, Boys and Girls of Wake-Up Town, Broadcasting Health, Health School on Wheels, Health and Success,* and *Health and Good Citizenship.* As one recalls the dreary story of health in the books of the past, one has reason to envy the child of today who studies these entertaining books with their interesting text and attractive illustrations.

Edgar A. Cockefair of the Central Missouri State Teachers College, assisted by Ada Milam Cockefair, a specialist in physiology, wrote *Health and Achievement,*

[241]

which appeared in 1936 and aroused the interest of the children and of the teachers of the subject.

Two great schools are represented in a college textbook on physiology entitled *The Human Mechanism* — namely, the Massachusetts Institute of Technology, through Theodore Hough and William Thompson Sedgwick, and the University of Virginia, through James A. Waddell.

Another college textbook, looking to a larger grasp of the problems of human adjustment, is *Fundamentals of Health*, the work of T. Bruce Kirkpatrick of Columbia and Alfred F. Huettner of New York University. This book is an advanced treatment of the human organism, covering physiology, hygiene, human origins, and human life-processes.

Good citizenship is the backbone of the nation, and from its beginning the house has endeavored to promote the cause. In 1886, as we have seen, appeared *Our Government*, written by Jesse Macy of the University of Iowa.

In 1918 Grace A. Turkington, a research student, wrote a book on civics entitled *My Country*, which received the endorsement not only of teachers but also of men in public life for the charm of its style and for its power to inspire pupils to strive for high ideals and noble actions.

In the ever-widening field of economics, especially with the national welfare as its goal, Dr. Thomas Nixon Carver of Harvard and Dr. Maude Carmichael of Arkansas State Teachers College, in their *Elementary Economics*, discuss the increasingly active part of the government in economic life, and offer a program for the common good. Production, distribution, capital, labor, exchange, money, and commercial crises are treated at length.

Dr. Frederick B. Garver of the University of Minnesota and Alvin Harvey Hansen of Harvard, in their new and substantial volume *Principles of Economics* for college students, cover the field of social and private economy and the social legislation of recent years. The book presents the story of production, value, money, and prices, the distribution of wealth and income, and international economic relations. It is a compendium of the economic activities of the day in business, government, and the home.

For high schools Dr. Howard C. Hill of the University High School, the University of Chicago, wrote (1922) *Community and Vocational Civics*, to present to the pupil an understandable treatment of the economic, social, and civic aspects of good citizenship; for it has been said that the major job of a member of a democracy is that of citizenship. To carry out his vigorous presentation, Dr. Hill prepared readings in community and vocational life. In 1935 appeared his latest book, *Life and Work of the Citizen*.

Agriculture has been called the oldest science in the world and the youngest. It is certainly the most important, for man must directly or indirectly live from the soil. In view of the fact that the farm population of the United States is nearly thirty-two millions, one quarter of the entire population of the nation, it is not to be wondered that new courses of agriculture are being taught and that a new science of agriculture is being developed. The first book to meet this need was Burkett, Stevens, and Hill's *Agriculture for Beginners*, a notable success for the house. *Essentials of the New Agriculture*, by Dr. Waters, inspires a love of rural life and, at the same time, teaches the most approved methods of farming.

In *Modern Agriculture*, a revision of Dr. Waters's *Essentials*, we have a popular survey of agriculture. The titles are familiar: corn, wheat, small grains, legumes, sorghum, tobacco, cotton, potatoes, fruits, livestock, poultry, farm machines and the soil, the world's treasure house. The authors are Dr. Grimes and Dr. Holton of the Kansas State College of Agriculture and Applied Sciences. These authors maintain that agriculture is never finished. What was good practice yesterday may be obsolete tomorrow. They show how the farm may be a place of beauty and of charm.

The entrance of the United States into the World War was a matter of grave concern to all publishers, as it was to businessmen in general. A rationing of paper was put into effect by the Federal government. This cut down to a marked degree the output of the Press. That its workers might be as fully employed as possible, the firm used its quota of paper to the limit, not only in the production of books already on the list, but even in the publication of new ones to meet the future demands of the schools after the war. All employees in offices and in the Press who were enrolled under the colors were guaranteed their positions at the return of peace. When the families of the workers who were at the front were in want, the salaries of the absent workers were paid to the families.

After the armistice, when once more the men were back again at their work, a banquet was extended to them. Mr. Stevens of the editorial department, who had gone to France for the war, tells the story of this banquet. He writes:

" From my whole connection with the firm, one of the occasions that I remember with the greatest satisfaction was the dinner tendered to all of us who had returned from the army to our positions with the firm in Cambridge and Boston. The party was at the Boston City Club. The Boston partners, acting in the name of the firm, had invited to be their guests the seventy-five or so men from the Press and the Boston office who had returned safely from the World War, and every man, if I remember correctly, was present on the occasion. Dr. Lawler had come from New York to deliver the principal address.

" More than one feature of the dinner and the speaking that followed was memorable, particularly the generosity of the partners in presenting a gold watch,

[245]

suitably inscribed, to each of the seventy-five guests. I have carried mine ever since and have often exhibited it with pride.

" But the high light of the occasion was Dr. Lawler's address. We had expected that he would tell us what fine fellows we were, and, in general, give us the pat on the back that we had had from many, as our military service was gradually brought to a close. Instead of that commonplace and facile sort of praise, his talk was upon the significance of the struggle in which we had just had a part. He spoke with great eloquence and on the same intellectual level as though to a group of college professors. Every man present I think was aware of the compliment. Instead of talking down to us, he was raising us to the philosophical level from which he, as a historian, viewed the conflict. All round me I felt and heard appreciation of the compliment that this implied. Every soul present seemed to respond. It was unforgettable."

CHAPTER THIRTY

◊

THE WORLD OF BUSINESS

IN THE late eighties a decided trend in the schools from cultural to commercial subjects was nearly everywhere in evidence. To meet this new condition, the house published in 1891 Gay's *Business Bookkeeping*, written by the superintendent of the Malden schools, Massachusetts. Some years later (1902) George W. Miner of the Westfield (Massachusetts) High School presented a manuscript. With John H. Moore (a teacher of great ability and head of the commercial department of the Charlestown High School of Boston) as co-author, the book was published as the *Moore and Miner Accounting and Business Practice*. It was followed by *Practical Business Arithmetic*, later revised by Miner, Elwell, and Touton. These books enjoyed a wide success in the rapidly developing commercial studies.

To meet the needs of this important field, an assistant editor was appointed, and Clarence H. Lingham, a graduate of Brown University, was given charge of the department. In 1917 Powers and Loker presented a manuscript entitled *Practical Exercises in Rapid Calculation*. It was planned by the authors to be in the form of a pad, a radical departure for the house, which at the time did not look with favor on that type of publication. To their surprise, however, it was a great success, the sales running into three quarters of a million copies in the following years.

Succeeding the Moore and Miner text came *Principles of Bookkeeping*, a revision by Miner and Elwell.

[249]

With this book the name of Fayette H. Elwell of the University of Wisconsin, later to become so important as an author, appears for the first time on Ginn and Company's list. In 1926, in collaboration with James V. Toner, an instructor in commercial subjects at Boston University, Elwell wrote the Elwell and Toner Bookkeeping and Accounting Series. Subsequently he wrote *Bookkeeping for Today*, a text which was widely adopted by schools throughout the country and which carefully combined modern theory and practice with sound teaching technique.

To present a different approach, *Bookkeeping and Business Knowledge* was accepted and published. Its authors were J. Hugh Jackson of Stanford University, Thomas Henry Sanders of Harvard, and A. Hugh Sproul of the State Teachers College, Salem, Massachusetts. To Dr. Sanders was dedicated the *1937 Yearbook* of the Harvard Graduate School of Business.

Every field of business activity—typewriting, graded dictation, elementary economics, secretarial training, occupations, retail selling, modern business English, business and correlated arithmetic, economic geography, business training, business law—has been covered for Ginn and Company by such noted teachers as Rowe, Bogert, McMackin, Korona, Carver, Marsh, Egan, Brewer, Carmichael, Caseman, Newman, Baten, Goodman, Edelson, Norton, Davis, Spanabel, Colby, Foster, Veit, Beighey, Hurlbut, Durand, Getchell, Cooper, and Stone.

In an article on wider horizons for social business it was said:

" It is important to know in this practical day that it costs six cents an ounce to send a letter by air mail; it is important, too, to be able to interpret a time table correctly, to make a bank deposit, to reconcile a monthly bank statement, and to do a hundred and one other things which are incidental to the business of living and working in this modern world. But it is likewise important, and this fact has been too largely ignored in the traditional courses in junior business training, to see to it that the student who is being introduced to business practices does not get lost among the trees and so fail to discover the woods."

A move of decided progress toward wider horizons was the publication in 1937 of a new series as well as a new type of textbook, *How Modern Business Serves Us* and *Business: Its Organization and Operation*, books designed to teach the pupils economic intelligence and how business benefits society, how it is organized, and how it affects the individual. Six authors, experts in commercial education, co-operated in writing this series: Dr. William R. Odell of Oakland, California; Dr. Harold F. Clark of Columbia University; Guy D. Miller of Springfield, Massachusetts; Oscar B. Paulsen of Hayward, California; Dorothy L. Travis of Grand Forks, North Dakota; and Ruth M. Twiss of Newton, Massachusetts. The wide and interesting sweep of these books, presenting information so important to every pupil as a future individual in business and as a member of society, may be best illustrated by the attractive and suggestive titles of the parts. In the first volume: " Communicating Ideas in the Modern World "; " Travel in the Modern World "; " Transportation in the Modern World "; " Handling Money and Sharing Risks "; " Budgeting and Spending." In the second volume: " Business and How It Is Owned and Directed "; " The Financial Background of Business "; " Raising Money for a Business and Safeguarding the Investment "; " Methods Used in the Buying and Selling of Goods and Services "; " Business in Its Relation to Society."

The Elwell bookkeeping books were, so to speak, forerunners of Ginn and Company's latest publication in bookkeeping — *Personal and Business Record-Keeping*, by Elwell, Zelliot, and Good. With Elwell are associated Ernest A. Zelliot, at present director of commercial education, Des Moines (Iowa) public schools, and Harry I. Good, associate superintendent of schools for secondary education, formerly director of commercial education, Buffalo, New York. These three authors have had unusually wide experience in teaching, supervising, and accounting. Their book not only presents business bookkeeping but also shows to what extent the personal and social uses of bookkeeping have become important factors in modern life.

CHAPTER THIRTY-ONE

◇

THE INCREASING HISTORY LIST

THE HISTORY LIST for elementary schools has been actively developed to meet the increasing attention given to this subject in present-day progressive schools. In 1892 Montgomery published his *Beginner's American History*, an interesting biographical study of the leaders in our national life. With a new *Elementary History* his list was complete.

As early as 1902 there appeared the first of the Lawler American histories, *The Essentials of American History*. This text was followed by six others, to carry on the history work from the primary through the grammar grades. In 1933 appeared the *Standard History of America*. The *Gateway to American History*, giving the European background, has been translated into Spanish and is widely used in the schools of Spanish America.

In 1928 Ginn and Company published *Teaching American History in the Middle Grades of the Elementary School*, written by Mary G. Kelty, who had been supervisor of history in the State Teachers College of Oshkosh, Wisconsin. On reading the book, superintendents and teachers realized that a new prophet had arisen in the field of elementary history.

The book made so instant an appeal that the company asked Miss Kelty to prepare a series of textbooks based on the ideas in her teachers' guide. In her interesting series Miss Kelty leads the child from the paleolithic age to the development, in North America, of American civilization and government.

[255]

The Tryon and Lingley History Series is the work of Dr. Rolla M. Tryon of the University of Chicago and the late Charles R. Lingley of Dartmouth College. Assisted by Frances Morehouse of Hunter College, they wrote the *American Nation Yesterday and Today*, a text that bespeaks the ripe experience of years of study and teaching.

The widening influence of history is well illustrated in the publication of books showing the influence of an Old World background on our culture and present being. History in American schools no longer begins with the landing of the great explorer Columbus in the Bahamas. We are the heirs of the ages. Kelty's *How Our Civilization Began* and *The Old-World Beginnings of America*; the *American People and Their Old World Ancestors*, by Grace Vollintine of the Francis W. Parker School of Chicago; *Adventures in Old World History*, by Hattie L. Hawley of the State Teachers College, Fitchburg, Massachusetts; Jeannette Rector Hodgdon's *The Enchanted Past*; Atkinson's *Introduction to American History* and *European Beginnings*; Walter Taylor Field's *Finding the New World*; and Lawler's *Gateway to American History*, all show the ever-broadening view of history since Cheyney's masterpiece, *European Background of American History*. In 1929 Dr. Long, student of nature and of English literature and history, assisted by Elizabeth C. Coddington, research scholar, published for the grammar grades *Our Country*, a drama of living men and women.

[256]

ILLUSTRATIONS SUCH AS THIS AID HISTORY TEACHING

To meet the special needs of the great metropolitan school system of New York City, Dr. John E. Wade and William E. Grady, associate superintendents of schools of the city of New York, co-operated with Miss Kelty in writing *The Story of America's Progress* (in six volumes) to meet the requirements of the grades from four to six.

Some years earlier, in another branch of the curriculum, the firm invited Dr. Gustave Straubenmüller to write *Home Geography* for the New York City system.

A better selection of an author could not have been made. Dr. Straubenmüller had risen from grade teacher to the high office of associate superintendent of schools. One of the earliest and most earnest advocates of nature study in the country, he promoted, with vigor, the School Art League. He was one of the nation's leaders in vocational education.

CHAPTER THIRTY-TWO

◇

HIGH–SCHOOL ENGLISH

IN THE YEAR 1922 William M. Tanner, who had had wide experience in the teaching of English in high schools wrote for the house his *Composition and Rhetoric*. This was followed seven years later by his *Correct English*, designed for the ninth grade. This book had a success beyond that of any similar text of its day. For the seventh, eighth, and ninth grades Briggs, McKinney, and Skeffington, specialists in junior-high-school subjects, wrote the series called Junior High School English. Lyman, Johnson, and McGregor continued their elementary Daily-Life Language Series into the junior high schools. Gaston, Chapin, and Nagelberg, all of the New York City high-school system, give in their *English in Daily Life* a thorough training in composition, basing their work on the present-day experiences of the pupil. Dr. Francis K. Ball, in his charming books *Building with Words* and *Constructive English*, sets forth the interesting story of the building up of the English language and its correct usage. When there is a romance in word origin, these books present it to the pupil. The books are authoritative; for Dr. Ball is a master in the matter of English derivation and usage. " English composition," he says, " is not dull, nor indefinite, nor insurmountable. Indeed, it may be made to lead to new and loftier vistas, by a path which is surprisingly easy, direct, and alluring."

He illustrates the growth of language and of words and tells what words should be accepted and what rejected. He is, perforce, compelled to bow at times to the acceptance of words that custom ordains, as sanctioned by Horace two thousand years ago:

si volet usus,
quem penes arbitrium est et ius et norma loquendi.
Epistulae, II, iii, 71–72

Charles Harlow Raymond, head of the English department in the Lawrenceville School, New Jersey, has, like Dr. Ball, a deep respect and reverence for words. In *A Book of English* he not only treats grammar and the usual mechanics of the subject but also develops the use and mechanics of words. In an interesting paragraph he writes as follows:

" Words are like people. They belong to families, and often they are very old and proud families. Some words are hundreds of years old; some, thousands of years. Some, like *wind* and *bread*, have belonged to our first families from the earliest times; others, like *cane*, just as proud, have sought us from afar. Three thousand years ago, perhaps more than four thousand, *cane* was a reed on the bank of the Alpheus River in Greece. From there he moved to Rome some two thousand years or so ago. After Caesar conquered Gaul, he traveled into the France of today. From there, filled with an insatiable curiosity or love of adventure, he crossed the English Channel, perhaps with William the Conqueror's host. Now in our country he is very far removed in time and space from the glamour of Greece, and few of us suspect

[262]

how varied and interesting a life this proud, unobtrusive citizen of the world has lived. And *cane* has grown in power and influence today. If you don't believe it, look him up in his home in the dictionary."

Valuable aids toward eliminating errors in the speech of high-school pupils have been given by Guiler and Henry in their *Remedial English*. Miss Nelle Button gives in *Creative English* a training in observation of nature and of human beings, and offers suggestions for recording these observations correctly, interestingly, and succinctly.

As early as 1886 Professor John F. Genung of Amherst College presented to the company a manuscript on rhetoric, which was accepted at once and published as *The Practical Elements of Rhetoric*. Scholarly teachers welcomed the book as an unusual contribution and a pioneer influence in the subject. It was noteworthy for its keen, sympathetic, and searching analysis, and full of inspiration for the student. One teacher wrote that the critic is conscious of a feeling of surprise as he misses the orthodox dullness. Many years after the publication of the book the New York *Nation* said, "For most college graduates of the last fifteen years, Genung has been a name to conjure with."

The *Handbook of Rhetorical Analysis* was published to accompany the textbook. Genung based his *Handbook* largely on the writings of Matthew Arnold and Cardinal Newman as exemplars of English undefiled.

Genung's treatment was a revelation to the teaching world. The book struck a new note. The effect of Genung's point of view has shown itself in every textbook on the subject that has appeared since the publication of his books.

In 1916 Dr. William J. Long, author of charming stories of nature, wrote *English Literature*, which gives not only the history of English literature but also its significance for the life of the English-speaking world. Mr. Long, who received his doctorate in philosophy at Heidelberg, brought to his work his inimitable style as well as his keen insight, his enthusiasm, his mastery of words, and a warmth of feeling for the beauties of English literature. He believes that to understand an age or a people we must read not simply their history, which records their deeds, but their literature, which reveals the dreams that made these deeds possible. *English Literature* was soon followed by *American Literature*. To accompany the texts, readings in both books were prepared by Dr. Long and Miss Wheeler, a research student.

For many years Brother Leo of the Order of the Brothers of the Christian Schools has charmed audiences in California with his brilliant analysis of current works of literature. He is professor of English literature at Saint Mary's College, whose bells re-echo over the beautiful Moraga valley. Brother Leo enjoys a broad classical culture. In his *English Literature* he traces, from the earliest days in ancient

Britain, the growth of English letters to the present time. His charm of style and informative text cannot fail to inspire the pupil with a love of literature and of all that is beautiful.

To show that literature of inestimable value may be a world-wide possession of the earnest student, William L. Richardson and Jesse M. Owen, in *Literature of the World*, really cover the world. Writers who penned their works on the banks of the Indus or the Liffey, or among the fiords of Norway, or under the shadow of the Kremlin, or in England or Spain or Italy, are all represented here in an interesting survey.

For a deep study of correct English usage Arthur G. Kennedy, professor of English philology at Stanford University, answers in his *Current English* the many questions about what is, and what is not, correct English usage. In 1930 appeared *Masters of Nineteenth Century Prose*, a scholarly work by Joseph J. Reilly, Ph.D., of Hunter College.

To aid the student in securing a broader and more varied reading program, Good Reading for High Schools was prepared by Dr. Tom Peete Cross of the University of Chicago, Dr. Reed Smith of the University of South Carolina, and Elmer C. Stauffer of the Crane Technical High School of Chicago. The four volumes of the series cover the entire four years' work in reading in the high school. In his *English Prose and Poetry* Professor John Matthews Manly of the

University of Chicago gives to the colleges an anthology of the best in English literature from the period of old English to modern times. In *The Literary Essay in English* Sister M. Eleanore of Saint Mary's College, Notre Dame, Indiana, presents the essay as a vital contribution to the culture of the college student.

In their *Types of Poetry* Professor Howard Judson Hall of Stanford University and Professor John Robert Moore of Indiana University offer the college undergraduate a rich collection from English and American authors, recognizing fully the poets of today.

Highroad to English Literature, a graphic story of English literature, was published in 1935. In it Elizabeth Collette of the Peabody High School of Pittsburgh gives the pupils a new survey-course, with a historical and social background and generous information about authors and their works. With nine literary maps, there is no reason for the pupil's wandering far from his path; and with the carefully prepared bibliography he can study for himself the growth of our language and literature.

For a recent point of view in American literature the house published in 1936 *Literature and American Life*, by Professor Percy H. Boynton of the University of Chicago. In a picture of the life of our people, as reflected in their own literature, drama, songs, and ballads, it presents the literature of the Revolution and of the succeeding epochs, with numerous references and supplementary studies.

CHAPTER THIRTY-THREE

◇

BROADER SUBJECTS

THERE is an unmistakable tendency in the schools to group the materials of instruction in broader fields of subject matter. This point of view is definitely expressed by the committee which prepared the *Twenty-sixth Yearbook of the National Society for the Study of Education.*

The Committee of Twelve experts on the curriculum (Dr. Harold Rugg, chairman) presented a joint statement from which the following passage is taken (Part II, p. 22):

" It is impossible to initiate pupils into an adequate understanding of world affairs without assembling in close relationship such facts, movements, and generalizations as those which deal with natural resources, economic imperialism, international diplomacy, world-trade, nationalism, and the like. These facts and generalizations are now scattered in the several separate subjects of geography, political history, economics, industrial and social history, and the like. These and other illustrations indicate the necessity of grouping in broader units much material that is now distributed through several distinct school-subjects.

" This proposal does not imply the mere merging or fusing of the present content of existing school-subjects. It implies, on the contrary, that the materials of instruction should be assembled from the starting point of the needs of the learner, irrespective of the content and boundaries of existing subjects. Where the needs of the learner in one field demand new subject-matter or make the use of subject-matter from another field desirable, the present content of the subjects and the divisions of the subject-matter should not be permitted to act as barriers to the improvement of instruction. There is nothing sacred about the present content and organization of the various subjects."

In its simplest elements this report means the disregarding of subject lines and the integration of the sequences of history, geography, and civics. These are presented, not as separate subjects, but as a progressive, interwoven course, showing, indeed, the relationship between them, but overstepping the boundaries which up to that time had presented a clean-cut differentiation. To the simple triple subjects mentioned above were at times added elementary economics and elementary sociology, for the enrichment of the curriculum, and the broader aspects of our social living; also at times homemaking, a study of modern civilization, anthropology, economic geography, and a history of the State in which the school system is located.

Some of the fused courses ranged from the earliest appearance of man and his conquest of nature, through the story of the classic nations, the medieval period, and the development of the present era. In most cases the curriculum, seeking a broader informational background, asks for a much wider use of libraries, museums, newspapers, magazines, periodicals, and other reference works, combining these extra activities with the school curriculum.

When the problem of fused courses in the junior high schools was presented to the firm by Dr. Harold Rugg, the proposal was accepted as a welcome aid to the enrichment of the social program in the schools. The plan involved a wide range of publications, not only suitable texts but comprehensive workbooks, teachers' guides, and tests.

Dr. Rugg, who has been the most distinguished leader of the fusion idea, graduated at Dartmouth with the degree of Bachelor of Science. He received from the same college a degree in engineering. The University of Illinois gave him the degree of Doctor of Philosophy. Since 1920 he had been professor of education in Teachers College, Columbia University.

As an engineer, a professor of education, and a student of history and psychology, Dr. Rugg brought to the study of the problem of the social sciences, a study which began more than two decades ago, a background that was invaluable. He mastered the salient points of a problem engaging the active attention of advanced workers who were experimenting in the new social-science movement in the Horace Mann School and in San Antonio, Fond du Lac, Rochester, San Jose, Cleveland, St. Louis, and many other school systems, all apparently agreeing with Dr. Giddings's suggestion that the ultimate aim of all society is to produce social personality.

[271]

Dr. Rugg could not accept the ideas proposed or sanctioned by the various educational societies and associations as to the worth of organized subject fields. He insisted on a fuller recognition of the relation of social science to the everyday life of the average citizen. He maintained that the subject matter should be organized in units of experience which approached as closely as possible to actual situations.

He began to lay the foundations of his work by preparing pamphlets, which were subjected to the critical judgment of active-minded, progressive teachers. The pamphlets, covering grades seven, eight, and nine, were tested for a number of years in classroom work in hundreds of schools, to determine if they were socially useful and pedagogically sound. They were revised from time to time, as new data were discovered by means of classroom experiment.

When at last the period of experiment was at an end, Dr. Rugg began the publication of his epoch-making books, a panoramic view of world society, whose very titles were a challenge to the existing order.

Combined with the pupils' workbooks, the series presents a compelling study of social science. That Dr. Rugg is not static, to use a now familiar term, is evident from the fact that he has studied the results of his textbooks for the past eight years, and has already begun their revision. *An Introduction to American Civilization*, the first volume of the series, becomes, in revised form, *Our Country and Our People*, a book which gives a graphic picture of the United States: the story of its immigrants, its regional geography, its economic problems, and its standard of living in comparison with that of other nations.

A comparison of the new edition with the old shows graphically the rapidity of the progress of events.

Dr. Rugg and Louise Krueger, director of the Walt Whitman School of New York City, believe that the social-science course is best approached through correct and interesting storytelling.

To meet this need, they have published The Rugg Social Science Series for elementary schools.

In the initial volume, *The First Book of the Earth*, the child starts on a ride through space. Carried on a magic cloud, he sees in the distance the earth rushing on its course, with the sun, moon, and millions of stars moving in their orbits. He watches the changing processes of day and night and the evolution of the seasons. There are revealed to him, as he travels, continents, mountains, oceans, rivers, and volcanoes in the process of formation. He reads stories and myths. He has before him a picture of life in its simplest forms, and watches the development of plants, trees, glaciers, giant animals, men of the Ice Age, and cave-dwellers — a story of science in a most attractive aspect.

Four additional volumes have been published: *Peoples and Countries*; *The Building of America*; *Man at Work: His Industries*; *Man at Work: His Arts and*

Crafts. The eighth and final volume of the elementary course is a résumé called *Mankind Throughout the Ages*. In the eight volumes of this series the child is, though unconscious of it, already within the realm of geography, history, economics, sociology, anthropology, drama, and aesthetics. With the workbook, his activities are given wide play during the development of his mind.

The elementary social-science hour has become for the child a pleasant anticipation. With the texts which Ginn and Company have had the foresight to prepare for him, the child who enters the third grade has an uninterrupted social-science course extending to the second year of the high school.

Another series in elementary science that interests the child and gives him new worlds to discover as he looks about him is Craig's Pathways in Science series, which covers six of the nine grades, as recommended by the *Thirty-first Yearbook of the National Society for the Study of Education*. Through this plan elementary science is not mere play, but an essential part of the curriculum.

When Dr. Gerald S. Craig of Teachers College, Columbia University, was preparing for his series, he invited to co-operate with him the following progressive teachers, specialists in the field of elementary science: Sara E. Baldwin of the Oak Lane Country Day School; Agnes Burke, Beatrice Davis Hurley, and Margaret G. Condry, of the Horace Mann

[274]

Elementary School; and Goldie M. Johnson, supervisor of elementary science in Montclair, New Jersey. These specialists, knowing the teacher's needs, instituted a careful study of the reactions of children to elementary science, and tested in the classroom the tentative course of study that had grown out of extensive researches. The result is the Pathways in Science series, six texts rich in content and in suggested easy scientific experiments. The books also suggest things to think about and things to do, thus leading the pupil to wider and more interesting activities and opening the world of elementary science to his eyes and mind.

Of the greatest importance to the child is the fact that what he has learned about science in this series is, though elementary, so accurate that he never has to unlearn it except as modified by newer discoveries or researches.

An important step was taken for junior high schools with the publication of A Survey of Science, which makes a continuous series with Pathways in Science.

The *Thirty-first Yearbook* had recommended that the science courses of the seventh, eighth, and ninth grades should be considered as an integral part of the program of instruction in science for the periods of elementary and secondary education. The science on this level should, on the one hand, be built upon and comprehend the science of the first six grades; on

[275]

the other hand, for those pupils who continue in school beyond the ninth grade it should serve as a basis for the special sciences of the high school and the orientation into them. Above all else, it must provide the most useful experiences in science that are possible for the pupils on this level, and it must be in accordance with the acceptable objectives of a liberal education for boys and girls from twelve to sixteen years of age.

The series A Survey of Science, a three-year integrated program with directed activities, was written by Samuel Ralph Powers and Herbert B. Bruner, professors in Teachers College, Columbia University, and Elsie Flint Neuner, supervisor of elementary science in New Rochelle. This series plans to arouse the scientific interest of pupils in the world about them by showing how all living things are dependent upon one another and upon their physical environment.

Three books, *The World Around Us*, *This Changing World*, and *Man's Control of his Environment*, present a continuous program for general science throughout the three years of the junior high school, presenting in graphic narrative style both physical and biological science.

Fortunate indeed are those pupils whose teachers have had in their training the rich background given them by the study of this unusual series.

In An Introductory Course in Sience for Colleges, Frank Covert Jean, Ezra Clarence Harrah, and Fred

Louis Herman, all of the Colorado State College of Education, joined with Dr. Powers in a two-book series which throws an interesting light on man and his relations to the physical universe and to the biological world. Chemistry, physics, meteorology, geology, and astronomy bring to these chapters the story of their newest development. Space, the cosmic bodies, the hydrosphere and the atmosphere, changes in the earth's surface, the modification of man's activities by science and the development of living organisms, the Mendelian theory, the control of disease, and man's cultural development, are some of the topics presented to the earnest student in a form that beckons him onward to ever-deeper study and more careful research.

CHAPTER THIRTY-FOUR

◇

THE FIRM ENLARGED

Some years ago Mr. Parkhurst sought an assistant who would relieve him of much of the detail connected with the firm's finances, which, along with the care of the Athenaeum Press, had become a task of heavy moment.

Allen Leach Priddy was recommended to him by the authorities of Dartmouth College, and he was promptly engaged. Priddy graduated from Dartmouth in 1915 and from the Amos Tuck School of Finance the following year. He became an instructor in that school, and its secretary.

After a period of financial activity with two large business concerns not far from Boston, he entered the firm of Ginn and Company to assist in the treasurer's department. From the outset of his school life Priddy had shown a remarkable aptitude for finance and mathematics, an aptitude which manifested itself at once in his quick, wonderful grasp of the manifold details of publishing. He showed also a keen appreciation of the agency side of the business, the more remarkable because he had never been an agent.

He served as assistant treasurer for a time and later as treasurer of the house. He was admitted to partnership in 1922. In the midst of his brilliant business life he died suddenly at a college banquet in 1935. To Priddy one might well apply the words of Milton,

"Lycidas is dead, dead ere his prime,
Young Lycidas, and hath not left his peer."

[281]

In 1910 a new agent was enrolled on the Ginn list, Millard Henry Jencks, born in heroic Herkimer County, New York, where, during the Revolution, colonists fought and won the important battle of Oriskany. It was natural that a university in the north country should appeal to Jencks. He went to St. Lawrence University, where he graduated in 1905. For four years he was connected with the school system of Troy, New York. While teaching here he studied law and was admitted to the bar of the State of New York; but, as fate would have it, he did not enter the profession. He resigned from school work to become an agent for the house for a decade in western New York.

In 1918 he entered the service of the nation in the World War, serving at Camp Upton, Long Island. After the war he came to New York City to take up high-school and college work, covering agency work in New Jersey, Virginia, and North Carolina with remarkable success.

One of the subjects he taught in his early high-school days was mathematics, a subject which has stood him in good stead; for upon it he built up a wide knowledge of existing business-processes and financial enterprises. He became a trustee of St. Lawrence University and, after a few years, chairman of the board, a position to which he brought a wide knowledge of educational progress and business acumen of a high order.

He was admitted to the firm in 1923, and on the retirement of Mr. Hodgdon he took over the high-school and college work in the State of New York. Taking charge of the work in Canada, he established an office in Montreal for the house's rapidly extending business throughout the Dominion.

The successor to Dr. Thurber in the editorial chair was Ernest Nichols Stevens. Stevens was born in Maine, where he received his early education, fitting him for college. He graduated from Harvard in 1903. He received an appointment in the Philippines in the Bureau of Civil Service, where he remained until 1912.

The Philippine service was under the strictest regulations, and merit alone counted in appointment or promotion. The work was interesting and stimulating to a degree, since it covered all branches of the service. Stevens had to prepare, or oversee the preparation of, questions for thousands of applicants, and the examination of the ratings.

After his long colonial experience in the distant isles of the Orient, Stevens came home on leave, and soon received an appointment to the agency work of the house, covering, at the outset, parts of Canada and of the South, where he showed himself remarkably well equipped. In a short time he became an assistant to Dr. Thurber in the editorial department.

During the World War he enlisted in the tank corps and entered camp at Gettysburg. In the silent watches of picket duty he walked up and down the lines held by the blue and the gray fifty-four years before, when the Confederacy pushed for a decisive thrust into Northern territory in the early days of July, 1863. Going to France, he was stationed at Cohons, not far from Dijon. In his leisure hours Mr. Stevens wandered through the neighboring ruined breastworks thrown up by the great Julius Caesar, whose custom it was at all times to protect his position carefully, as we see in his famous *Commentaries*.

At the close of the World War, Stevens resumed his work in the editorial department. He was admitted to the firm in 1928.

To the arduous position of editor he brought an unusual equipment. His early training on a farm gave him a correct view of the life in the country; he saw the panorama of history in college and war days; he learned in the Orient how other peoples live and have their being; he studied in his agency work the relation of the publisher to the needs of the classroom.

As editor, he judges with rare acumen the manuscripts that come to him, and knows well what subjects need new texts and what the texts should be to meet these needs. In his office he continues the same kindly relations between publisher and author as Dr. Thurber maintained in his long service as editor.

Some years ago the writer of this book happened to be in New Orleans. It was a beautiful Sunday afternoon in May, with the magnolias, poinsettias, and bougainvillias in full bloom. There he met Robeson,

(STANDING) S. C. SMITH, L. H. GRIFFIN, L. J. WEED, S. W. NEWELL, H. C. LUCAS, E. H. KENERSON, A. L. PRIDDY, N. C. MILLER, H. H. WOOD

(SEATED) T. B. LAWLER, C. H. THURBER, E. N. STEVENS, L. PARKHURST, L. B. ROBESON, G. A. PLIMPTON, M. H. JENCKS, H. H. HILTON, M. R. JOUETT, O. J. LAYLANDER

(STANDING) F. A. RICE, H. H. WOOD, H. C. LUCAS, B. R. BUCKINGHAM, E. K. ROBINSON, W. S. GIRLING, S. W. NEWELL, L. H. GRIFFIN, J. C. AMBLER

(SEATED) S. C. SMITH, O. J. LAYLANDER, C. H. THURBER, E. H. KENERSON, H. H. HILTON, M. H. JENCKS, T. B. LAWLER, E. N. STEVENS, L. J. WEED, M. R. JOUETT

who presented to him a new agent named Samuel William Newell. Newell was born in Georgia. He graduated at the University of Mississippi, and became superintendent of schools at Tupelo, from which position he came to the firm.

The group that May afternoon was joined by the principal of one of the large high schools of New Orleans and by Justin H. Smith, who at this time was spending his days with the Spanish archives.

The five started on a type of pilgrimage. They went first through the old French quarter, with its foreign-looking streets, much quainter then than now. They visited the old Cabildo, with its wonderful collection of mementos of days harking back to the times of the Spanish viceroys. The group stood almost in awe at the Place d'Armes, in memory of that day in 1803 when the French tricolor, coming down from the top of the flagpole, met, at the halfway point, the American flag as it slowly rose. Both flags stopped for a moment, as if in salute. Up to the top now ascended the Stars and Stripes, and the vast Louisiana Purchase, a veritable empire, was ours. McMaster gives us a graphic picture of the scene.

Then our pilgrims examined the interesting levees, which hold back ol' man river. And now, all the time afoot, they reached the battlefield where Old Hickory repelled in decisive victory the tried veterans of Great Britain, a victory that paved the way for Jackson's election to the presidency of the United States.

Newell had come down from northern Mississippi to take charge of agency work in the group of states along the Gulf of Mexico. He was admitted to the firm in 1931, and now directs the work in a large part of the Southern States, with headquarters in Atlanta.

The death of Dana Hall left a vacancy in the directorship of the high-school and college work in the Chicago field, and Harry Hinds Wood was appointed to fill it. Wood was born in Iowa, and graduated at Grinnell College. He became a teacher and principal of schools in towns of his native State. In 1910 he was recommended for the agency force of the house by Laylander, who had charge of Iowa and had seen Wood at work there. He was engaged by Dana Hall.

Wood represented the high-school and college department in the State of Wisconsin. Here he remained until 1931, when he was called to Chicago to take up Dana Hall's work. In 1933 he was admitted to the firm.

The extent of the high-school and college work in a field as large as that of Chicago is exceedingly wide and complex. The West is decidedly progressive, and is ever on the alert for the most advanced ideas in the field of education. Wood has given continued study to the problems of his field and is ever striving to widen his intellectual horizon. His knowledge of textbooks is profound. He has been a great asset to the firm in strengthening its position in the high schools and colleges of the West.

Another partner was added to the firm in 1933, Lee Henry Griffin, who was born in Wisconsin. Griffin graduated at the University of Chicago and carried on advanced work at Columbia University. He had experience in teaching, both in the elementary school and in the high school. From teaching he became an agent of Ginn and Company.

Upon the declaration of war by the United States in 1917, Griffin volunteered, going to Fort McPherson, Georgia. After twelve months in camp he was sent to France, where he served for fourteen months, to the end of the war. One day during his service he had a great surprise. The colonel in charge, who had served in the Boxer Rebellion in China, summoned Griffin to his tent and placed first-lieutenant bars upon his shoulders. The colonel had by cable recommended to the War Department, Washington, this promotion from sergeant to first lieutenant.

After a period of study at the University of London, Griffin returned to this country, where he again took up agency work, working at times in fourteen States of the West. He was brought to Chicago to assist Laylander. Upon Laylander's retirement he became Conway's assistant, and upon Conway's death his successor in charge of the elementary-school work in Chicago. In 1933 he was admitted to the firm.

As early as 1906 the rearrangement of the Columbus office, which covered the important States of Ohio, Kentucky, and West Virginia, brought into the agency field John W. Swartz, a graduate of Ohio Wesleyan University. In 1917, after years of active work as an agent, Mr. Swartz became a partner in the firm, and remained in charge of the Columbus territory until his retirement in 1930.

Swartz was succeeded by Homer C. Lucas, who was born on a farm in Highland County, Ohio, and graduated from the high school the very year that the World War broke out. He taught school, entered the war service of the nation, and later graduated from Ohio Wesleyan University.

His war work was with the United States Marines, in which body he was instructor in infantry drill. He describes the training in the camp as designed to develop self-confidence. Signs at the camp read, " If you don't know, you get killed." On the training-field, in the practice trenches, this sign was before the youthful soldiers. Knowledge is power, it seemed to say, in war as well as in peace.

In his later textbook adoptions that sign inspired Lucas to know his own books and the books of his competitors; to know the conditions likely to be met, the nature of the school curricula, the trend of education in general so far as it might at the time be knowable. In 1933 he became a partner.

In this volume the story of a certain meeting of the firm in Columbus has already been told. At this meeting Dr. Burdette R. Buckingham was invited to set forth his ideas on readers on an entirely new plan.

[288]

At this time Dr. Thurber wished to secure an assistant in the editorial department, especially for the elementary-school section. Dr. Buckingham's nation-wide reputation for all-round knowledge of elementary education as well as of research and psychology was well known to the firm, and he was invited to become a member of the editorial department.

The invitation was accepted, and Dr. Buckingham began his work with special reference to common-school publications.

Dr. Buckingham has been connected with education for the greater part of his life. He began teaching at the early age of seventeen, and since that time he has been engaged in teaching, research, writing, and editing. The only interruption was the years taken out to go to Wesleyan University, where he received his bachelor's degree. He received his doctorate in philosophy from Teachers College, Columbia University.

Dr. Buckingham was a grammar-school principal in the New York City schools. Later he became chief statistician in the same system and educational statistician for the Department of Education of Wisconsin. When President James of the University of Illinois invited him to organize a Bureau of Educational Research, he went to Champaign, where he remained for three years, until he was invited to Ohio State University for similar research.

The plan for his unusual series of readers, The Children's Bookshelf, had in the meantime been carried to completion, and met with instant success. For several years, in addition to his work for Ginn and Company, he taught in the Graduate School of Education of Harvard University. He became a member of the firm in 1936.

Edward K. Robinson was born in New Hampshire, and later became a resident of Massachusetts. Mr. Robinson graduated at Dartmouth College in the class of 1904. He entered the house's employ in the fall of that year, and during the following years covered the elementary schools of New England as agent, especially the schools of Vermont and Massachusetts.

Robinson had a wide and valuable experience in agency work in the progressive schools of northern Illinois. Returning to Boston, he became the manager of the art and advertising sections of the editorial department. To him fell the task of selecting artists, able specialists in their own fields, and of procuring pictures for textbooks covering so many branches of human knowledge. Before passing to other work, Mr. Robinson gathered together a staff which today carries on the traditions of the house for attractive textbooks, with illustrations that are not mere embellishments, but incentives to a better grasp of the subject on the part of the pupils. The modern textbook is a contribution to knowledge and also to art.

Mr. Robinson was admitted to the firm in 1937 and at the same time was made assistant treasurer. In 1938 he became treasurer to succeed Mr. Kenerson.

In 1937 the rapid growth of the firm's work on the Pacific coast led to the admission of Frederick A. Rice to membership. Mr. Rice was born in New Jersey, in the historic county of Monmouth, famous in the days of the Revolution. He is descended from old colonial settlers who moved to New Jersey from Connecticut. As a boy, Rice added to his visible but moderate wealth by picking tomatoes and berries for the neighboring sturdy Dutch farmers.

Moving to Brooklyn, he graduated from the Boys' High School, where he won a scholarship for Cornell University. Despite the fact that he earned his entire way through college, he received in his junior year his Phi Beta Kappa key. He graduated at Cornell in 1908. After a short business experience in New York City, he was happily appointed by Cornell to a fellowship in American history. Called to the Everett High School, on Puget Sound, near Seattle, he took up the work of teaching history. After two years he entered the firm's Pacific-coast office. His agency work covered almost an empire, all the Pacific states and the far-flung Territory of Hawaii. After twenty-five years of active agency work he became a member of the firm.

Wallace Sedgwick Girling, who became a member of the firm in 1937, was born in Jamaica, Long Island. He graduated from Union College, and in the next few years engaged in various types of business. In April, 1917, he enlisted for the World War. In 1922 he became an agent for the house, in both the common-school and the high-school field, where his success led to a partnership in the firm.

Another member added to the roster of the firm in 1937 was James C. Ambler. Mr. Ambler comes from Virginia. He was born on a large livestock farm in Fauquier County, eight miles from a railroad, with dirt roads almost impassable in winter except on horseback. He attended Washington and Lee University. While he was at this university the United States entered the World War.

Ambler volunteered in an ambulance company and was sent to France. After attending the Officers Training School at Saumur, France, he received a commission in the Field Artillery. He saw service in the Argonne Offensive. He also served in the Army of Occupation on the Moselle River, in Germany. After the war was ended he took courses in the University of Virginia.

A few years after his return he became superintendent of schools of Fauquier County. In 1929 he became a Ginn agent, covering especially a portion of the South until he was admitted to the firm.

Donald D. Grindell, a native of Wisconsin, graduated at the University of Wisconsin in 1910. After agency work for the firm in Minnesota, Wisconsin, and Indiana, he went to Kansas, where he resided until he took charge of the Dallas office with a wide territory covering the southwestern part of the

DONALD D. GRINDELL

NORMAN G. S. INGRAM

country, the storied land of Spanish missions and great plains, Navajos and Pueblos, Coronado, and the Grand Canyon. In 1938 he was admitted to the firm.

Norman G. S. Ingram was born in Edinburgh, Scotland. He entered the University of Glasgow as a student of applied science, deciding that engineering was his vocation. In vacation periods he worked in the great shipyard at Clydebank.

The World War interrupted his university course, and for a time he was engaged in building naval vessels. As soon as possible he enlisted in the navy.

After the war he returned to the University of Glasgow, from which he graduated. Later he accepted a position in the West Hill High School, Montreal.

In 1929 he became an agent for the firm. In 1933 an office was opened in Montreal to cover the great expanse of the Dominion of Canada, and Ingram was placed in charge. In 1938 he became a member of the firm.

IN CONCLUSION

A

B

C

EVER since the invention of printing, printers and publishers have used distinctive printer's marks, or colophons, as they have sometimes been called. These are now generally employed in a decorative manner on title pages.

For nearly fifty years Ginn and Company had no distinctive printer's mark. Various symbols produced by different artists had been used. These generally included the conventional lamp of learning, the head of Athena, or an open book.

In 1914 Mr. T. M. Cleland, an artist and typographical designer in New York, was employed to create a suitable mark for the firm. He very happily hit upon the hornbook as an appropriate symbol for Ginn and Company. Since 1914 the firm has used variations of Mr. Cleland's design in its publications.

Of the forms shown on page 296, *A* and *B* in several sizes and variations have been used in most of the firm's publications. The form marked *C* was made for use in special cases where a more or less ornate design is appropriate.

In this printer's mark the hand holding the hornbook typifies the service performed by the firm in offering textbooks for the education of youth; and the decorative branches of laurel and oak, with their conventional symbolism, provide a graceful setting for the hornbook.

The hornbook as a primitive form of the textbook would be an appropriate symbol for any educational publisher; but it was especially appropriate for Ginn and Company, since at the time Mr. Cleland designed this mark, Mr. Plimpton, then one of the senior partners in the firm, had been successful in adding to his private collection of old textbooks more specimens of original hornbooks than were to be found in any other public or private collection.

◇

As was said in the preface of this work, it has not been possible to present the story of the many books published by the house in its long existence. It is hoped that these pages give at least a somewhat worthy view of the wide sweep of the activities of a firm engaged in publishing textbooks, the interesting problems it tries to solve, and the even more interesting personalities that have had a part in building up for the firm the respect of the educational world during the past threescore years and ten.

INDEX

[301]

Mullins, G. W., 157
Munroe, L. B., 54
Muzzey, D. S., 172, 180
Myers, P. V. N., 72

Nagelberg, M. M., 261
Neesima, J. H., 60
Neuner, E. F., 276
Newell, S. W., 285
Newman, S. K., 250
Newton, E. W., 56, 221
Norton, C. E., 20
Norton, J. K., 224
Norton, M. A., 224

Odell, W. R., 251
Osias, C., 138
Owen, J. M., 265

Pahlow, E. W., 177
Palm, F. C., 181
Parkhurst, Lewis, 69, 86, 91, 234, 281
Paulsen, O. B., 251
Peattie, R., 198
Periodicals, 45
Perry, E. D., 42
Peters, C. J., 87
Philbrick, J. D., 53
Philippine Islands, 131–138
Philosophical Review, 48
Plimpton, G. A., 59–62, 72, 88, 143, 158, 231
Plimpton, H. E., 88
Plimpton, H. M., 88
Political Science Quarterly, 47
Potter, M. C., 145
Power, T. F., 195

Powers, E., 249
Powers, S. R., 276
Priddy, A. L., 281
Puerto Rico, 70, 125, 152
Pulsifer, W. E., 85
Purcell, R. J., 179

Raymond, C. H., 262
Rebmann, V. L. F., 221
Reeve, W. D., 157
Reilly, J. J., 265
Religions, Handbooks on the History of, 49
Revelli, W. D., 221
Rice, F. A., 291
Richardson, W. L., 265
Righter, C. B., 221
Robeson, L. B., 233
Robinson, E. K., 180, 197, 290
Robinson, J. H., 167
Rowe, C. E., 250
Rufi, J., 224
Rugg, H., 269, 271
Russell, H. R., 214

Saucier, W. A., 224
Schlauch, W. S., 157
Schurman, J. G., 45
Seymour, T. D., 40
Sharland, J. B., 56
Sherman, N. H., 214
Shimer, H. W., 198
Shoemaker, L. M., 215
Siceloff, L. P., 157
Skeffington, F., 261
Smith, D. E., 155
Smith, D. V., 172

Smith, E. P., 172
Smith, J. H., 69–71, 90, 113
Smith, Reed, 265
Smith, S. C., 227
Smyth, W. S., 71, 111
Spanabel, E. E., 250
Stauffer, E. C., 265
Steiger, G. N., 181
Stevens, E. N., 245, 283
Stevens, F. L., 244
Stewart, J. Q., 214
Stewart, O. M., 215
Stiles, L. B., 199
Straubenmüller, G., 257
Struthers, A. B., 224
Sumner, W. G., 199
Swartz, J. W., 235

Tanner, W. M., 261
Tarr, F. C., 122
Thatcher, T. A., 29
Thomas, H. G., 194
Thomas, R. S., 149
Thurber, C. H., 71, 149–151
Tippetts, C. S., 201
Toner, J. B., 250
Touton, F. C., 163, 224
Towne, J. R., 215
Toy, C. H., 50
Travis, D. L., 251
Trusts, era of, 95
Tryon, R. M., 256
Turkington, G. A., 242
Turner, F. J., 180
Turner, W., 200
Twiss, R. M., 251

Umstattd, J. G., 224

Veazie, G. A., 56
Veit, B., 250
Vlachos, N. P., 181
Vollintine, G., 256

Waddell, J. A., 242
Wade, J. E., 257
Waldron, R. A., 224
Walker, J. C., 180
Ware, E. W., 172
Warren, S. D., 25, 87
Waters, H. J., 244
Webb, W. P., 183
Weed, L. J., 235
Weinschenk, G., 89
Welchons, A. M., 162
Wells, C. G., 86
Wenckebach, C., 120
Wentworth, George, 157
Wentworth, G. A., 62–66, 156
Wheeler, M. L., 264
Whitcomb, H. C., 87
White, H., 200
White, J. W., 39
White, S. S., 101, 149
Whitney, W. D., 42, 121, 143
Wiehr, J., 120
Willard, R. C., 180
Williams, M. W., 182
Williams, R. F., 212
Wood, H. H., 286

Young, C. A., 214
Young, E. F., 188